OSPREY AIRCRAFT OF THE ACES • 93

RAF Mustang and Thunderbolt Aces

SERIES EDITOR: TONY HOLMES

OSPREY AIRCRAFT OF THE ACES • 93

RAF Mustang and Thunderbolt Aces

Andrew Thomas

OSPREY
PUBLISHING

Front Cover
On 8 March 1945 Norwegian ace
Lt Col Werner Christie arrived at
RAF Hunsdon, in Hertfordshire, to
lead the wing that comprised Nos
154 and 611 'West Lancashire' Sqns.
Both units were equipped with the
superb Mustang IV, flying them on
long-range fighter escort missions
for RAF Bomber Command 'heavies'
hitting targets in daylight raids.
Christie soon began leading the wing
in his personal aircraft that bore his
initials WHC, as was the privilege of
his position. The fighter (KH790) also
had a red spinner that Christie
recalled 'made my aeroplane a little
easier to spot and formate upon after
a dogfight or ground attack'.

A little over a month later on
16 April Christie, flying KH790, led
the escort for a Lancaster raid on
Swinemünde. When the bombers
were safely on their way home he
took No 611 Sqn down on a strafing
sweep, initially flying to the east of
Berlin where they encountered
Soviet Ilyushin Il-2 *Shturmoviks*
escorted by Yak fighters. After
exchanging recognition signals with
the Red Army Air Force pilots, he led
the unit back over Berlin. At 1750 hrs
near Finow airfield, northeast of
the enemy capital, some 20+ short-
nosed Fw 190 fighters were spotted
above the Mustang IVs at 10,000 ft.
Christie closed on one of the Focke-
Wulfs, describing what happened
next in his Combat Report;

'I opened up, firing a five-second
burst at the leading aircraft in a
formation of three, range 150 yards,
and observed strikes on the port side
of the engine and cockpit, and also
that his starboard wingtip was
damaged. The aircraft then began
to smoke badly and glide straight
ahead. I pulled out to the port side
and made a second attack, opening
up at 200 yards and again closing
in to about 50 yards, ending up dead
astern. I fired several short bursts
lasting ten seconds, and during
the attack I observed strikes on the
cockpit, engine and both wings.
The fighter's port wing fell off and
the port undercarriage leg fell down,
after which it did five or six quick
rolls horizontally and crashed in
flames in a wood.'

Others pilots from No 611 Sqn
were also engaged, and in what
proved to be the Auxiliary
squadron's last action of the war,
four more Fw 190s were destroyed.
Christie then reformed his wing and
led it back to England. The 27-year-
old Norwegian ace had just claimed
his tenth, and final, victory. It was
also the last aerial kill credited to
an ace flying an RAF Mustang.

This specially commissioned
painting by Mark Postlethwaite
shows the port wing of Lt Col
Werner Christie's final victim
starting to detach as the Focke-Wulf
fighter begins to spin away to its
destruction

First published in Great Britain in 2010 by Osprey Publishing
Midland House, West Way, Botley, Oxford, OX2 0PH
44-02 23rd St, Suite 219, Long Island City, NY 11101, USA

E-mail; info@ospreypublishing.com

© 2010 Osprey Publishing Limited

ISBN 13; 978 1 84603 979 9

Edited by Tony Holmes
Page design by Tony Truscott
Cover Artwork by Mark Postlethwaite
Aircraft Profiles by Chris Davey
Index by Fineline Editorial Services
Originated by PDQ Digital Media Solutions
Printed and bound in China through Bookbuilders

10 11 12 13 14   10 9 8 7 6 5 4 3 2 1

FOR A CATALOGUE OF ALL BOOKS PUBLISHED BY OSPREY
MILITARY AND AVIATION PLEASE CONTACT:

Osprey Direct, c/o Random House Distribution Center,
400 Hahn Road, Westminster, MD 21157
Email: uscustomerservice@ospreypublishing.com

Osprey Direct, The Book Service Ltd, Distribution Centre,
Colchester Road, Frating Green, Colchester, Essex, CO7 7DW
E-mail: customerservice@ospreypublishing.com

www.ospreypublishing.com

CONTENTS

EARLY DAYS

'A couple of miles short of landfall I spotted four Fw 190s off to our right at about 1500 ft. Their course and speed was going to put them directly overhead when we crossed the beach. I called Freddie twice with a "Tally ho!", but there was no response. He did not hear the warnings and apparently did not see the Fw 190s. When Freddie turned right to intercept our recce road at Abbeville, we were put in an ideal position for the FWs to attack. I swung very wide to Freddie's left during the turn, dusting the Abbeville chimney tops. That kept me beneath the FWs, and I believe they lost sight of me.

'My plan was to cut off the lead FW 190 before he could open fire on Freddie, but my timing went to pot when a crashing Spitfire forced me to turn to avoid a collision. That gave the lead FW pilot time to get into a firing position, and he hit Freddie's Mustang with the first burst. I got a long-range shot at the FW leader but had to break right when his No 2 man had a go at me. The No 2 missed and made the big mistake of sliding to my left side ahead of me. It was an easy shot and I hit him hard. His engine caught fire, and soon after it started smoking and the canopy came off. I hit him again and he was a goner, falling off to the right into the trees.

'The second pair of Fw 190s had vanished so I raced towards Dieppe looking for Freddie's Mustang. I saw him heading for the harbour at 1000 ft, streaming glycol, with the lead FW trailing behind. The FW started to slide dead astern Freddie, so I gave him a short high-deflection burst to get his attention. He broke hard left into my attack, and the ensuing fight seemed to go on forever. I could out-turn him, very slowly gaining an advantage, but just as I got into firing position he would break off and streak inland, using the superior power of his BMW engine. He would come back at me as soon as I turned to head for the coast, and we'd start our turning competition all over again. During one turn I had to dodge a crashing aeroplane – an Me 109 – and the FW pilot got his only shot at me. His deflection was too great and he missed. My opponent was a highly competent pilot, and I was ready to call a draw as soon as I could.'

Thus did American Plt Off Hollis Hills of the Royal Canadian Air Force's No 414 Sqn describe in the Summer 1990 edition of naval aviation journal *The Hook* how over Dieppe on 19 August 1942 he claimed the Mustang's first aerial victory. Hills later transferred to the US Navy and became an ace flying F6F Hellcats in the Pacific in 1944. This was No 414 Sqn's baptism of fire, and it went on to become the most successful of the Mustang reconnaissance units in terms of aerial victories.

The aircraft that Hollis Hills was flying that day was a product of a proposal by North American Aviation to the British Purchasing Commission (BPC) in early 1940. Having received US government sanction, the company went on to develop a very clean single-seat fighter design – the NA-73X – that received the US designation XP-51. It flew for the first time on 26 October 1940. This was an extraordinary achievement, as approval to proceed with the project had only been given

The first of the countless enemy aircraft shot down by the Mustang appropriately fell to an American serving in the RCAF, Plt Off Hollis Hills of No 414 Sqn. He later became an ace when flying F6F Hellcats with US Navy squadron VF-32 in the Pacific in 1944 (*Canadian Armed Forces*)

on 24 April! The BPC was impressed, authorising production of the aircraft for the RAF, which in December bestowed upon it the name 'Mustang'.

Powered by an Allison V-1710-39 engine, the first Mustang I was sent to the UK by sea in October 1941, where in flight trials it proved to be faster than the Spitfire V at 15,000 ft. However, its performance fell away sharply after that, as unlike the Rolls-Royce Merlin 45 in the Vickers-Supermarine fighter, the Allison engine was not supercharged. With substantial numbers of Spitfire Vs

available, the Mustang I's excellent range and low-level performance led to it being fitted with an oblique camera for use in the army cooperation role instead. Indeed, the fighter was gladly welcomed by Army Co-operation Command, which desperately needed a modern aircraft to replace the Tomahawk IIs then in service.

The Mustang I entered operational service on 5 January 1942 when No 26 Sqn, based at RAF Gatwick, in Surrey, received AG367 for operational tests. The unit received two more examples the following month. More squadrons were also issued with Mustang Is through the spring, and on 10 May Flg Off Dawson from No 26 Sqn flew the Mustang I's first operational sortie when he strafed the airfield at Berck-sur-Mer. The unit flew its second operation on the 14th when it photographed a radar site in the Pas de Calais – an unglamorous task that was nevertheless vital in the planning for the invasion of France in 1944. Gradually, the pace of these fighter-reconnaissance operations over occupied Europe increased, with No 239 Sqn becoming the next unit to declare itself operational with the Mustang I in June.

The first major action for the aircraft in RAF service came during Operation *Jubilee* on 19 August. This was a large scale raid on the port of Dieppe, and it led to some of the heaviest air fighting of the war. The four Mustang squadrons of No 35 Wing – Nos 26, 239, 400 and 414 Sqns –

No 414 Sqn Mustang Is like AG427/RU-H formed part of Army Co-operation Command from early 1942, undertaking tactical reconnaissance missions over occupied western Europe (*No 414 Sqn Records*)

One of the first RAF units to fly the Mustang I was No 4 Sqn, which was also equipped with the cannon armed Mk IA – this example was photographed in 1943 (*J D Oughton*)

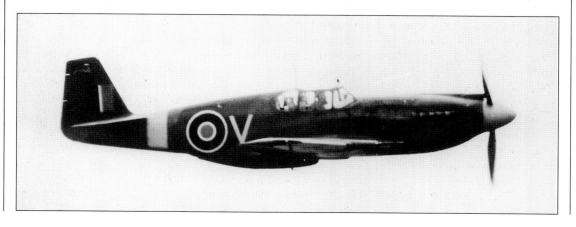

One of a number of aces that later flew Mustang Is in the army co-operation role was Flt Lt Glyn Griffiths of No 4 Sqn, who is seen here when still a sergeant pilot with No 17 Sqn in 1940. He was badly injured in a mid-air collision in 16 October 1943 (*M Goodman*)

flew in support of *Jubilee* throughout the day, blooding the new fighter in air combat for the first time as has already been described in this chapter.

As well as reconnaissance missions, the expanding force of Mustang I squadrons also regularly mounted more offensive sorties in the form of 'Rhubarbs', 'Rangers' and 'Populars'. These led to occasional brushes with the Luftwaffe, and a steady stream of losses mainly to light flak.

One of the most successful of these early army co-operation pilots was Flg Off Frank Hanton of No 400 Sqn who, on 8 July 1943, shared in the destruction of an Fi 156 Storch. Then during a night 'Ranger' to Rennes airfield in the early hours of 15 August he caught a Bf 110 nightfighter in bright moonlight as it made its approach to land and duly shot it down, so achieving the Mustang's first night victory – Hanton also damaged a Ju 88 during the same mission.

Through the summer of 1943 a number of aces were posted into Mustang I units including Flt Lt Bob Doe who, on 31 August, flew his only operational sortie with No 613 Sqn when he led a search for some refugee boats in the North Sea. Another was Flg Off Glyn Griffiths of No 4 Sqn who on 1 August flew a reconnaissance of the Cherbourg area. However, when returning to Odiham from a sortie over France on 16 October his wingman collided with him and he was badly burned before he could bail out of his stricken fighter, spending much of the rest of the war having treatment for his dreadful injuries.

The most successful army co-operation pilot in air combat was Canadian Flg Off Gordon Wonnacott of No 414 Sqn who soon after lunch on 2 November left RAF Redhill, in Surrey, with Flg Off Brown on a reconnaissance mission over Belgium. They attacked and damaged several locomotives and also a goods train. Then when in the vicinity of Cambrai Brown spotted two Fw 190s at zero feet crossing from left to right. Wonnacott related his actions after having turned to attack them;

'I started to attack the starboard aircraft but could not close until it turned into "Blue 2", who was attacking the port Fw 190. I saw strikes on the Fw 190 being attacked by "Blue 2", and as he overshot, the fighter I was chasing turned into "Blue 2" and I instructed the latter to break into him. I then closed in on the Fw 190 that "Blue 2" had overshot, opening fire at 250 yards and closing to 150 yards, observing strikes on the fuselage. The enemy pilot waggled his wings as I started to fire, and when I broke off the attack he turned over onto his back and went straight into the deck. I pulled away in a tight turn to find the other Fw 190 heading for home.'

Wonnacott's shared victory started him on the path to acedom. On 28 January 1944 during a 'Ranger' to the Chartres area, his section spotted a pair of Ar 96 advanced trainers. One exploded when hit by a burst of fire from Flg Off R O Brown and the second was downed in flames by Wonnacott in AP211 and Flt Lt Burroughs in AM251. They then encountered Bf 109Es from JG 105, and although Brown went down, Burroughs and Wonnacott each destroyed one. Gordon Wonnacott went on to 'make ace' after No 414 Sqn re-equipped with Spitfire IXs.

FIRST ACE

When delivered, in spite of the reservations about its high altitude performance, the new Mustang I naturally drew the attention of Fighter

Command, and examples were duly delivered to the Air Fighting Development Unit (AFDU) at RAF Duxford, in Cambridgeshire, for trials and comparative testing. The pilots of this unit were all highly experienced, and in June 1943 the famous one-armed ace Sqn Ldr James Maclachlan joined the AFDU following a lecture tour in the US.

On 29 June, in company with Flt Lt Geoffrey Page (who had 2.5 victories to his name), Maclachlan flew an offensive sweep over France. Leaving RAF Lympne, in Kent, at 0915 hrs, they crossed the Seine and when northwest of Rambouillet they spotted a number of aircraft, as the AFDU records noted;

'Over a wood the northwest of the town they sighted three Hs 126s at 2000 ft in line abreast. Sqn Ldr Maclachlan attacked the port aircraft, which caught fire after a burst of about two seconds from all guns. The aircraft flew for about three miles on fire and crashed into a house. Then a dogfight ensued with the other two, one of which Sqn Ldr Maclachlan attacked until it glided down into a wood. Flt Lt Page downed the third. It also crashed in the wood after a two-second burst from dead astern at a range of about 300 yards. No one bailed out of any of these aircraft.

'The Mustangs flew on for about ten miles and then sighted another Hs 126 doing circuits at about 2000 ft. Sqn Ldr Maclachlan fired a short burst which caused the enemy aircraft to take evasive action. It was then attacked by Flt Lt Page, who saw strikes. It half-rolled and dived into a field near Limours. Wreckage was strewn all over the field. They then flew on to Bretigny and saw two Ju 88s circling the aerodrome with wheels down, one at 2000 ft and one at 1000 ft. Sqn Ldr Maclachlan attacked the aircraft at 2000 ft and saw strikes and broke away, and then Flt Lt Page closed in and attacked. The Ju 88 crashed outside the aerodrome.'

In sharing in its destruction, Geoffrey Page had became the first of many Allied pilots to become an ace when at the controls of a Mustang. The pair were not yet finished, as on turning back they saw the second Ju 88 about to land. Maclachlan attacked it and the bomber immediately caught fire and crashed on the edge of the airfield. Having shot down six enemy aircraft between them, the pair then returned home from the most successful Mustang sortie to date.

The first pilots to claim multiple victories in an RAF Mustang were assigned to the elite AFDU. One of them was one-armed ace Sqn Ldr James Maclachlan, whose four claims on 29 June 1943 took his total to 16 and 1 shared destroyed (*via B Cull*)

A STAR IS BORN

Soon after the Mustang I's arrival at the AFDU in the spring of 1942, it was noted by Rolls-Royce chief test pilot Ronald Harker after he flew the aircraft that 'with a powerful and good engine like the Merlin 61, its performance could be outstanding'. Further discussions took place with the recommendation that aircraft should be thus fitted for testing in Britain that summer, and that a variant of the Merlin built in the US by Packard such as the V-1650-3 be fitted and tested in a P-51A in America.

The first flight of a Merlin-Mustang subsequently took place in the UK on 13 October 1942, and the aircraft generally performed well. In the US the first flight was undertaken at North American's Inglewood, California, facility on 30 November, with the second one being flown in February 1943. An order for 2000 examples of the new variant, designated the P-51B, had been placed even before the prototype's first flight, and they entered service with the USAAF and RAF in late 1943. A star had been born.

D-DAY AND 'DOODLEBUGS'

The first USAAF P-51Bs to reach the frontline were delivered to the 354th Fighter Group (FG) in the UK in November 1943. On 22 December No 65 Sqn accepted its first Merlin-powered Mustang III at RAF Gravesend, in Kent, and by the end of January 1944 the unit was operational. No 65 Sqn was led by eight-victory ace Sqn Ldr Reg Grant, who was promoted to lead Mustang III-equipped No 122 Wing shortly after his unit returned to operations. He was in turn replaced by Sqn Ldr G R A M 'Robin' Johnston, who had claimed four victories in North Africa in 1941-42. Also joining No 65 Sqn at this time was New Zealander Flt Lt B G 'Buck' Collyns and the RAF's only Icelandic pilot, Flg Off T E 'Tony' Jonsson, who also had four victories to his name. Both men would 'make ace' on Mustang IIIs during the coming months.

No 19 Sqn also began re-equipping at this time, and on 15 February it combined with No 65 Sqn to perform the first Mustang III sweep, flying over Brussels and Lille. Future ace Flt Sgt Basilios Vassiliades noted in his logbook, 'Nothing seen. First fighter sweep by RAF Mustang IIIs'.

No 122 Wing's third unit, No 122 Sqn, was still re-equipping at this time, but among its pilots were Flg Offs Lance Burra Robinson and Maurice Pinches, both of whom were to achieve great success through the summer. However, on 28 February No 122 Wing suffered a great loss when, after taking off to lead a Marauder escort, Wg Cdr Grant suffered an engine failure in his fighter (FX996) and crashed into the sea off Gravesend. He thus became the first ace to be killed in a Mustang III. Grant's place was taken by Sqn Ldr Johnston, who was in turn succeeded by Kiwi ace Sqn Ldr D F 'Jerry' Westenra. The wing then gradually increased its operational tempo, flying sweeps and escorts in support of USAAF and RAF medium bombers and protecting anti-shipping Coastal Command Beaufighters over the North Sea.

Towards the end of March additional deliveries enabled the squadrons of No 133 (Polish) Wing to begin re-equipping at RAF Heston, in Middlesex, No 306 getting its first Mustang III on the 26th and No 315 on the 28th. The latter unit was led by 11-victory ace Sqn Ldr Eugeniusz 'Dziubek' Horbaczewski, and among his pilots were Sgt Jakub Bargielowski, who had suffered in a Soviet Gulag for some years, and seven-victory ace Flg Off Kazimierz Wunsche.

The wing's third unit was No 129 Sqn, whose CO was Sqn Ldr Charlton 'Wag' Haw. A very experienced pilot with four victories to his name, Haw had been awarded the Order of Lenin by the USSR for his actions during the Murmansk expedition in 1941. He told the author;

'We were given Mustangs just before moving to Heston, then on to No 133 Advanced Landing Ground (ALG) near Horsham, in Sussex.

Flt Sgt Basilios Vassiliades was with No 19 Sqn when it converted from the Spitfire IX to the Mustang III and flew on its first operation with the American fighter on 15 February 1944. By the time he was shot down in August Vassiliades had claimed five and two shared victories (*via C H Thomas*)

From there we did long-range escorts with B-17s to the Ruhr, and then on to Berlin – the latter missions took close to five hours to complete. Just before the invasion we used the Mustang for ground attack, taking two 500-lb bombs on board. I left the unit two months after D-Day, and on that day it was taken off offensive ops to chase V1s.'

Haw had several other successful pilots on strength with him at No 129 Sqn, including Flt Lt John Hancock, who had five and one shared victories, and Flg Off Desmond Ruchwaldy with seven kills. Elsewhere, the Polish manned No 316 Sqn at RAF Coltishall, in Norfolk, also began re-equipping for escort work.

On 1 April No 133 Wing moved to RAF Coolham ALG, in Sussex, and like No 122 Wing at nearby RAF Funtington, also in Sussex, it became part of the 2nd Tactical Air Force (TAF). Despite this organisational change, operations remained much as before. During a wing sweep to Strasbourg in the late afternoon of 22 April, Flt Sgt Vassiliades (in FB104) shot down a Bf 109 for his first kill, while on the same sortie Flg Off N E S Mutter (in FX944) claimed No 65 Sqn's premier Mustang III success when he too destroyed a Bf 109. Also victorious was Wg Cdr Johnston (in FX996), whose Bf 109 kill gave him ace status. His Combat Report stated;

'I sighted 14 Me 109s crossing my bow 400 yards below at about 15,600 ft. They were on my starboard side at a range of about 1000 yards. Almost immediately afterwards I saw the Hun leader jettison his tanks. I jettisoned mine and called out "attacking". I turned to port above them as they were also turning to port. After half a circuit they half-rolled. I chased them, and after three minutes began to overhaul the rear aircraft. I fired from dead astern, range about 250 yards, and saw strikes. He took me through some high tension cables, interrupting my firing. He was then incredibly low, and either his engine stopped or he throttled back. I put down 20 degrees of flap and closed in astern to 100 yards and gave him a long burst. Light smoke streamed out. Suddenly his nose dropped and he hit the side of a small valley and blew up.'

On 23 April No 122 Sqn, which had lost its CO to flak earlier in the month, also got in on the action during a 'Ranger' to Dole/Tavaux

The only RAF unit in No 133 (Polish) Wing was No 129 Sqn, to which Mustang III FB129/DV-F belonged. It was flown by several notable pilots, including seven-victory ace Flg Off Desmond Ruchwaldy. One of the longest serving Merlin Mustang IIIs, the fighter participated in No 129 Sqn's first operation with the type on 26 April 1944 and also flew in its last on 20 April 1945 (*Paul Hamlyn*)

The wing leader of No 122 Wing was Wg Cdr 'Robin' Johnston, who in claiming the first of his Mustang III victories on 22 April 1944 became an ace. His previous successes had come in Hurricane IICs with No 73 Sqn in North Africa in 1941-42 (*via C H Thomas*)

The four pilots from No 122 Sqn who on a 'Ranger' to Dole/Tavaux airfield on 23 April 1944 shot down six He 111s between them. They are, from left to right, Flt Lt L A P Burra-Robinson, Plt Offs E A Roemmele and J Crossland and Flt Lt A F Pavey. Both Burra-Robinson and Pavey would become aces flying the Mustang III by the end of the summer. The aircraft behind them bears the squadron marking on its nose (*ww2images*)

He 111H G1+MU was one of the victims of No 122 Sqn's devastating attack on Dole/Tavaux airfield (*ww2images*)

airfield, on the Swiss border. Four of the unit's Mustangs arrived at the base at the same time as eight He 111s, and in the one-sided action that followed six were shot down. Flt Lt Lance Burra-Robinson (in FZ164) began his road to 'ace-dom' when he shot down two bombers and shared a third with the rest of the section. He described his first two victories as follows;

'A He 111 crossed my path from "two o'clock" at about 300 ft. I broke into a position line astern of it and fired from 300 yards, closing to 200 yards, observing strikes first on the starboard mainplane close to the engine and then on the fuselage. The aircraft's nose dropped and the pilot appeared to attempt a crash landing. The aircraft skidded on impact, crashed through a hedge and the greater part of the starboard mainplane simultaneously dropped off. I had to break immediately as I saw another He 111 approaching. I broke into line astern, firing and closing from 250 to 100 yards. Strikes were seen on the mainplane and on the fuselage. Pieces flew off the aircraft, which dived nose first into a field, bursting into flames.'

Plt Off John Crossland (in FZ131) also shot an He 111 down and shared in destroying two others for his first victories. Also tasting success were Plt Off E A Roemmele (in FB110) and Flt Lt A F Pavey (in FZ168), who wrote;

'I attacked one which was just lowering its undercarriage. My range was approximately 250 yards and line astern of the aircraft. I saw strikes on the engine, and oil from the aircraft covered my windscreen. Weaving attacks had to be made due to the low speed of the bomber, and after several of these the starboard engine stopped and the starboard wing caught fire. The aircraft crashed in a field, simultaneously colliding with a tree. Three members of the crew got out and ran across the field.'

Having damaged another Heinkel, he then went for a third bomber that had already been attacked by the others;

'I attacked, hitting the fuselage, and on my second pass I stopped the rear gunner's fire – strikes were also seen on the starboard engine. This aircraft endeavoured to escape by flying very low and comparatively fast. I saw it blow up in the air and crash into a wood.'

The tempo of action continued to increase, with No 129 Sqn beginning operations and the numbers of claims steadily mounting. On 28 April – the day No 306 Sqn flew its first Mustang III mission – No 19 Sqn's Basilios Vassiliades (in FX955) claimed his second success

during a 'Ranger' to the Tours area. Sharing the kill with Flt Sgts W T Warren (in FB158) and A J Fellows (FZ181), he recalled;

'I flew line abreast and identified it as an Arado 96. I turned and fired from 300 yards, closing to 200 yards, from various angles. The aircraft took evasive action, and I eventually saw strikes in the cockpit after an attack from astern and above. The starboard undercarriage leg fell down and the aircraft hit the ground.'

On the last day of the month No 122 Sqn's CO, Sqn Ldr T H Drinkwater, led eight Mustang IIIs on a 'Ranger' that destroyed several training aircraft on the ground. Shortly afterwards he was replaced by a New Zealand ace from North Africa, Sqn Ldr Ernest Joyce.

With their confidence in the range of their Mustang IIIs confirmed, No 122 Wing was tasked with a 'Ranger' to an airfield in Aalborg, in northern Denmark, on 6 May. Nos 19 and 122 Sqns each sent a pair of fighters, and it proved successful. Lance Burra-Robinson (in FZ168) destroyed a Hs 129 on the ground, but Flg Off E L Germain (in FX955) of No 19 Sqn was in turn attacked by two Fw 190s and shot down and killed by Unteroffizier Lückenback of 10./JG 11. Despite this setback, the wing believed that this could be a fruitful area for further sweeps, and a repeat attack was duly suggested.

The following day withdrawal cover was given to a homeward bound USAAF raid by No 65 Sqn (led by Derek Westenra), the unit picking up the bombers just 70 miles west of Berlin.

No 122 Wing returned to Aalborg early on the morning of the 17th when Wg Cdr Johnston led eight aircraft from Nos 65 and 122 Sqns on one of the most successful Mustang III 'Rangers' ever flown. Having refuelled at RAF Coltishall, the aircraft flew at low-level across the North Sea in two sections – Johnston, Westenra, Collyns and Flt Lt R Barrett, with Lt K Nyerrod, Flg Off M H Pinches and Flt Sgts W P Kelly and R T Williams in 'Blue' section. They arrived over Aalborg at midday, where although achieving surprise, some Bf 109s and Fw 190s from 10./JG 11 did manage to engage them.

Mustang III FZ120/YT-J of No 65 Sqn sits bombed up awaiting its next sortie in the weeks before D-Day. The aircraft was regularly flown by unit CO and ex-desert ace Sqn Ldr Jerry Westenra, who shot down an Fw 190 in it on 8 June. FZ120 was also flown occasionally by fellow ace Flt Lt 'Buck' Collyns (*Mrs M Kidner via Stephen Darlow*)

The first section spotted a formation of Ju 88s from KG 30, and all four were shot down – Johnston (in FZ151), Westenra (in FZ120) and Collyns (in FX900) each claimed one, with all three sharing the other. However, enemy fighters arrived and Barrett (in FX993) was killed when he was shot down into the Lim Fjord by Unteroffizier Rudschinat. Barrett may have downed two Bf 109s prior to his demise.

To the south, 'Blue' section spotted two elderly Junkers W 34s, one of which Nyerrod (in FZ118) sent down in flames while future ace Pinches and Australian 'Ned' Kelly (in FZ125) despatched the second. Pinches then spotted two moored Ar 196 floatplanes, which he duly strafed. As he pulled up from his run, he spotted an He 177 that he promptly attacked. The huge bomber from 4./KG 100 exploded when it hit the ground west of Aalborg town. Pinches then attacked a Ju 88 over the airfield that also crashed inverted.

While this was happening, 'Ned' Kelly had positioned himself behind a Bf 109, but just as he was about to open fire he was baulked by another Mustang III (possibly the aircraft flown by Barrett), which set the fighter on fire. Kelly switched to a second Bf 109, shooting it down before firing on an Fw 190 that he claimed to have damaged. He then fired on what he thought was a Do 217, and saw one of the crew bail out – this was credited to him as a probable.

Kelly's fellow NCO Rowland Williams (in FZ110) was also in action, having damaged a W 34 before spotting three aircraft flying very low in line abreast that he thought were more He 177s. His fire hit one, but then another Mustang (possibly Maurice Pinches) also attacked, forcing him to break away. Williams' frustration was, however, momentary, as he then attacked a formation of three more W 34s and claimed two of them destroyed. As he pulled off to the north he spotted what he again identified as an He 177 (actually another Ju 88) and fired on it too. Williams saw the crew bail out of the blazing aircraft. However, as he described years later to the author;

'As I made my final attack from the rear, with flap set down so I did not overshoot, the pilot pulled the bomber's nose up. The lower gunner jettisoned something – possibly armour-plating – that got stuck in my air scoop, causing the engine to seize and the aircraft to almost stall. With no height to bail out I had to make a forced landing.'

Williams was almost immediately picked up by the Danish resistance, and after many adventures he reached neutral Sweden on 6 June. He was

The most successful Mustang III mission prior to D-Day was the 'Ranger' flown by No 122 Wing to Aalborg on 17 May. On this sortie Flt Sgt Rowland Williams shared in the shooting down of an 'He 177' (actually a Ju 88) and also destroyed a second 'He 177' and two W 34s. However, a piece of debris from his final victim struck FZ110/YT-S, forcing Williams to crash-land in Denmark. Sheltered by the Resistance, he eventually escaped via Sweden, and upon returning to his unit he received the DFM for his exploits (*R T Williams*)

Flt Lt Wladislaw Potocki (left) of
No 306 Sqn, who became an ace
during June 1944, discusses tactics
with another ace, Sqn Ldr Peter
Thompson of No 129 Sqn. The latter
had assumed command of No 129
Sqn from 'Wag' Haw in July 1944
(*Polish Institute and Sikorski
Archive*)

flown back to England by a BOAC
Mosquito on 2 July! For his exploits
on this epic fight in which he made
his only claims of the war, Rowland
Williams received an immediate
DFM upon his return.

As the long awaited invasion
of France approached, the Mustang
IIIs of both wings switched
to fighter-bomber duties. As the
intensity of operations increased
in the lead up to Operation *Overlord*,
other pilots began to open their
scores. One was the experienced
Flt Lt Wladislaw Potocki of No 306
Sqn, who had previously carried
out operational testing on the Spitfire XII. On 18 May he and three of
his squadronmates shared in the destruction of an He 111 northeast
of Nevers for his first success. Another was 21-year-old Australian WO
Max Bell (in FX943) of No 19 Sqn, who made his first claim on 21 May
when he helped shoot down a LeO 451 south of Viborg while escorting
a Mosquito raid. He noted in his Combat Report that after seeing a
Mosquito firing at it;

No 129 Sqn's first Mustang III CO
was Sqn Ldr 'Wag' Haw, who is
seen here sitting on his kit sharing
a joke with the unit's medical officer
upon their arrival at RAF Coolham
ALG in early April 1944. Haw had
previously been awarded the Order
of Lenin by the Russians for his
actions over Russia (*C Haw*)

'Wag' Haw's regular aircraft was
FB169/DV-H, which he flew many
times. On the evening of D-Day
he was at its controls when he led
fighter cover for airborne forces
landing in the eastern beach area
(*via C H Thomas*)

'I opened fire from 400 yards, closing to 250 yards. The enemy aircraft stuck its nose down, which brought me into line astern, and I continued firing and saw strikes on the port engine, which blew up. The port wing then fell off and the aircraft dropped away in flames.'

However, casualties were also mounting, with four Mustang IIIs being lost to various causes on the 20th and two more on the 21st. No 315 Sqn did its best to even up the score on 25 May when four of its pilots downed a pair of Ar 96 trainers near Bourges during a 'Ranger'. No 19 Sqn gained a new CO during May too when seven-victory ace Sqn Ldr W M 'Mac' Gilmour took over. On 1 June No 122 Sqn boss Ernest Joyce (in FX954) made his only claim on the Mustang III when he shot down an He 111 north of Alte Mellum, in the Frisian Islands, during a 'Ranger'.

D-DAY

Jusr prior to D-Day the aircraft of both wings had broad black and white Allied Expeditionary Air Force identity stripes painted around the wings and fuselage. On 6 June itself, No 122 Wing's squadrons formed part of the huge fighter force that escorted the second wave of troop carriers and gliders to Normandy. They then flew myriad ground support sorties for the invading troops, resulting in mounting losses to the enemy's deadly light flak batteries.

The Polish wing escorted glider trains in the evening, No 129 Sqn's 'Wag' Haw (in FB169) leading 11 aircraft to the eastern beach area near Caen. In a fight with Fw 190s of JG 26, Flt Lt John Hancock (in FZ121) and WO W E Rigby (in FB171) shared in the destruction of an Fw 190 – the sole victory claimed by Mustang IIIs on D-Day.

D+1, however, saw the wings involved in some intense aerial action, with 16 German fighters being destroyed for the loss of six Mustang IIIs. Among the successful pilots in the morning sortie was No 306 Sqn's Flt Lt Grzegorz Sologub (in FX873), who shot down a Bf 109 to claim his first Mustang III kill, and fourth success overall. In an early evening patrol squadronmate Flg Off Herryk Pietrzak (in FB111) was flying east of Argentan when he encountered some Bf 109s, one of which he shot down and damaged a second. Also successful was Flt Lt Wladislaw Potocki (in FZ196), as he too claimed a Bf 109 in the same action. Ten minutes later, in another combat some ten miles south of Caen, Pietrzak became an ace when he shot down another Bf 109, as did Potocki.

The following day No 65 Sqn was in the process of conducting an early bombing attack near Dreux when Fw 190s were spotted near the target

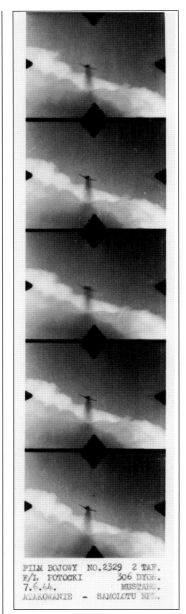

FILM BOJOWY NO. 2329 2 TAF.
F/L POTOCKI 306 DYON.
7.6.44. MUSTANG.
ATAKOWANIE - SAMOLOTU NPL.

These gun camera stills show the demise of one of the two Bf 109s shot down to the northeast of Nevers on D+1 by Flt Lt Wladislaw Potocki of No 306 Sqn (*Polish Institute and Sikorski Archive*)

When he gained his double 'kill' on 7 June 1944 Potocki was flying Mustang III FZ196/UZ-D, which is seen here landing fully bedecked in D-Day stripes at RAF Coolham ALG (*Polish Institute and Sikorski Archive*)

area. After a long chase at low level three German fighters were brought down. One fell to the guns of Sqn Ldr Derek Westenra (in FZ120), who described his final victory in his Combat Report;

'I overtook one '190 and opened fire at 600 yards. Throughout the chase the Hun did not weave, flying straight as the intervening contours permitted towards the east. I closed and fired numerous short bursts from different angles. I saw strikes and the engine stopped. Then the '190 pulled up to 800 ft and the pilot bailed out. The parachute opened. This was west of Dreux, 60 miles from where the chase had started.'

The steady stream of losses to flak continued, however, and one pilot brought down on 8 June was future ace Flt Lt Michal Cwynar of No 315 Sqn, who force-landed (in FB188) south of Caen but returned to his unit

Mustang III FB145/PK-F of No 315 Sqn is bombed up at RAF Coolham ALG just prior to D-Day. Flt Sgt Jakub Bargielowski used this machine to down two Fw 190s near Sens on 12 June, the fighter also being flown by Flg Off Jerzy Polak when he destroyed two Bf 109s 12 days later (*Polish Institute and Sikorski Archive*)

Sqn Ldr 'Mac' Gilmour, CO of No 19 Sqn, lays in relaxed repose outside his tent in early June 1944. Seated is fellow ace and CO of No 122 Sqn, Sqn Ldr John Shaw (*J W Bennett*)

safely. The weather deteriorated on 9 June, severely curtailing aerial activity, but the heavy fighting around Caen, in the British sector, against determined opposition continued unabated.

The following day Mustang IIIs from Nos 122 and 133 Wings were out over the front, and they had several skirmishes with marauding Bf 109s, suffering seven losses to these and ground fire. Amongst several pilots who registered claims in return were No 65 Sqn's 'Buck' Collyns (in FX900), who shot a Bf 109 down for his fourth victory. He noted in his Combat Report afterwards;

'I was bombing southwest of Caen when I heard "Presto Leader" call up and say he was being attacked by Me 109s with British markings. As we neared the area I saw an aircraft approaching from head-on, and at first presumed it was another Mustang joining up. Suddenly I realised that it was an Me 109. I immediately pulled round and dived, firing from 20 degrees to line astern. The aircraft caught fire, rolled onto its back and dived into the ground. I saw the pilot bail out and his parachute open.'

The action continued unabated, with ground attacks in support of the forces slowly expanding the beachhead. Typical was the sortie flown by future ace Flg Off 'Jimmy' Talalla of No 122 Sqn on the evening of 12 June when, during an armed reconnaissance, he bombed a train near La Queue les Yueliners.

Earlier in the day No 315 Sqn's Mustang IIIs had set out to bomb targets near Mortagne and spotted seven Fw 190s below them at very low-level. Flt Sgt Jakob Bargielowski (in FB145) shot down two of them for his first kills, his CO, Sqn Ldr 'Dziubek' Horbaczewski (in FB166), claimed the first of his six successes while flying the Mustang III and Flg Off M Kirste recorded the second of his three victories. This pattern continued for the next week or so as 2nd TAF units flew flat out to break the enemy in the critical fighting in Normandy.

During the late afternoon of 17 June No 122 Sqn again flew an armed reconnaissance, attacking a train. However, as they did so they were 'bounced' by three Bf 109s from IV./JG 27 and the CO, Sqn Ldr Ernest Joyce (in FX986), was shot down and killed. American Flg Off Jim Thorne (FX935) in turn destroyed one of the Bf 109s – probably the aircraft flown by *experte* Leutnant Ernst-Wilhelm Reinert, who bailed out – for his fourth victory. A short while later another section from No 122

Mustang III FB201/QV-D of No 19 Sqn shows the improved 'Malcolm Hood' to advantage. It was the regular mount of Sqn Ldr 'Mac' Gilmour, who was flying the fighter when he claimed his first Mustang III victory on 20 June 1944 – he also claimed his last victory in it too on 12 July. Flt Sgt Vassiliades claimed an Fw 190 and a Bf 109 destroyed, and an He 111 damaged on the ground, when flying FB201 on 24 June (*J D Oughton*)

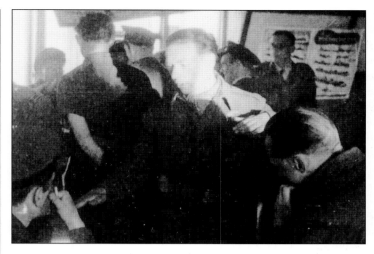

No 315 Sqn's Flt Sgt Jakub Bargielowski demonstrates to the debriefing officer how he damaged a Bf 109 over Tilliers on 24 June 1944 (*via Wojtek Matusiak*)

Sqn encountered two more Bf 109s near Dreux, as Maurice Pinches (in FZ114) recalled at the time;

'I got behind one at about 1500 yards. After approximately three minutes I got to within 1200 yards, so I gave it a couple of short bursts and a large flash was seen at the starboard wing root. I was not gaining rapidly, and at 500 yards, commenced firing again, many strikes being seen. When the range had closed roughly 200 yards the aircraft pulled up sharply, got rid of its hood, went over onto its back, did a couple of flat spins, then dived into the ground from a height of about 300-400 ft. The pilot bailed out at about 300 ft, his parachute opening 200 ft from the ground.'

The second Messerschmitt was shot down by the rest of the section. Joyce was replaced by another ace in the form of Sqn Ldr J T Shaw, who had 6.5 victories to his name, but his tenure was only for a few weeks.

The No 122 Sqn CO was not the only ace to fall victim to the enemy at this time, however, for on 22 June 'Buck' Collyns (in FB236), now with No 19 Sqn, was hit by flak and forced to bail out. He returned safely to his unit, but fellow ace Flt Lt John Hancock (in FZ121) was killed that same day when he was flying one of two No 129 Sqn Mustang IIIs to be hit by flak near Thiberville. Despite these losses, others continued to add to their scores in the skies above Normandy, including No 19 Sqn's Sqn Ldr 'Mac' Gilmour (in FB201) on 20 June, who gained his first success with the Mustang when he shot down a Bf 109 near Dreux and damaged another. Squadronmate Flt Sgt Vassiliades (FB368) also claimed a Bf 109 kill the following day.

MUSTANG ACES

By this stage a number of Advanced Landing Grounds had been established both in Normandy and along the south coast of England, and squadrons from both Mustang III wings prepared to move closer to the action. Without interrupting operational flying, No 315 Sqn moved to Holmsley South, in Hampshire, and strafed Panzers near Cherbourg on 22 June. Sadly, Flt Lt H Stefankiewicz (in FB398) was shot down by flak near Cherbourg and drowned in the Channel before he could be rescued, while in a now-famous incident WO T Tamowicz (in FZ147) crash-landed after also being hit by flak. He was then rescued by Sqn Ldr

Sqn Ldr 'Dziubek' Horbaczweski (right) and WO T Tamowicz flew back from France together in the former's Mustang III after the No 315 Sqn CO rescued him following Tamowicz's downing by flak in enemy-held territory on 22 June (*via Wojtek Matusiak*)

Horbaczewski, who landed and picked him up, both men returning in the Mustang III's small cockpit!

The following day No 306 Sqn celebrated the creation of its latest aces when at midday two sections were attacked by German fighters just as the Mustang IIIs approached their target at Verneuil. In the ensuing mêlée, aircraft from both sides went down, the Poles claiming seven destroyed. Two Bf 109s fell to the guns of Flt Lt Potocki (in FB168), who thus became the first RAF pilot to claim five kills with the Mustang III, while Flt Lt Sologub shot down an Fw 190 to also become an ace. However, five Polish pilots were lost in return, among them the CO, Sqn Ldr J Marciniak (in FX970), who was replaced by Sqn Ldr Pawel Niemiec.

No 122 Wing was again heavily engaged during an early morning armed reconnaissance on 24 June, with both Nos 19 and 65 Sqns encountering 30+ Bf 109s and Fw 190s in their target area southeast of Dreux. Leading his wing, Wg Cdr Robin Johnston bagged an Fw 190, while Flt Sgt Vassiliades (in FB201) was amongst the successful No 19 Sqn pilots. He noted in his flying logbook, 'Low-level bombing of railway near Evreux. 1 FW 190 destroyed, 1 He 111 damaged on ground, 1 ME 109G destroyed'. He was now just a half-kill away from becoming the second ace with five victories on the Mustang III.

No 122 Sqn's Flg Off 'Jimmy' Talalla (in FB224), a Singhalese who already had two victories to his name from 1943, gained his first on the Mustang III when he shot down a Bf 109, so continuing his path to ace status, while No 65 Sqn's Flg Off Tony Jonsson (in FZ112) shot down two Fw 190s to also become an ace. His squadron lost four aircraft, however, although three of the pilots evaded capture to return.

Later that evening it was the turn of the Poles to mount an armed reconnaissance, led by wing leader, the redoubtable ace, Wg Cdr Stanilaw Skalski (in FZ152). Having bombed a railway line, they were engaged near Tillieres by around 40 German fighters. Flying his personally marked fighter, Skalski claimed two (his only victories in the Mustang III), noting that the Bf 109 he attacked then turned and collided with a second one. Among the other successful pilots was Flt Lt Kazimierz Sporny (in FZ149) of No 306 Sqn who became an ace when he shot down a Bf 109 – he also damaged an Fw 190.

The following day No 122 Wing moved across to France to be based under canvas in the dust on the ALG at B7 Martragny, to the east of Bayeux. From there on the 27th, in unsettled weather, Wg Cdr Johnston led a patrol of No 65 Sqn aircraft to strafe some motorised transport, before finding enemy fighters and claiming his fifth Mustang victory;

'I made a rear starboard quarter attack on one '109 during a zoom, and after a burst which caused strikes along his engine and starboard wing root, he erupted in flames and was seen to go down by Flt Sgt Dinsdale. The pilot did not bail out.'

Near Bernay later that evening ten aircraft from No 122 Sqn spotted four Fw 190s and gave chase, Flt Lt Allan Pavey (in FZ167) recalling afterwards how he too became an ace;

'Opening fire from 800 yards using the gyro gunsight, I saw numerous strikes on the starboard aircraft. It fell to port streaming black smoke, caught fire and crashed in an orchard. The other three then broke, and I followed the leader into cloud. Breaking through into a gap in the cloud,

I saw the Hun 200 yards in front at an angle of 70 degrees. Giving a short burst again using the gyro sight, I saw strikes on the starboard wing. It folded back and came off.'

The Mustang III units of No 122 Wing faced a long, hard summer of fighting from the makeshift strips on the Continent. However, since the invasion the Germans had unleashed a deadly new threat against London and the southeast of England in the shape of the V1 flying bomb – more often referred to as a 'Diver' or 'Doodlebug'. A large number of high performance fighters were thus rapidly switched to counter this menace, among them No 133 Wing, whose transfer to France was postponed.

Mustang III-equipped No 316 Sqn, which had been conducting bomber escort operations from RAF Coltishall, was also allocated. At the beginning of July the latter moved down to RAF West Malling, in Kent, as the airfield was right in the path of the incoming pilotless V1s. Over the next two months the unit shot down 74 – more than any other of the Polish Mustang III squadrons, although it was 'pipped' as the most successful in the RAF by No 129 Sqn. It was a hazardous task, however, and in order to try to boost the Mustang's speed the use of 130 Octane fuel was experimented with, though with mixed results. These hazards were described by Flt Sgt Toni Murkowski, who recalled hunting his first V1 on 3 July to the author especially for this volume;

'We were based at Coltishall but the HQ moved us to Kent so we could provide the intercept aircraft, as reaction time had to be quick. Because the V1 was such a small target, our guns were harmonised for about 260 yards' range. I remember my first one – it was a foggy day, and most of the pilots had gone to the Officers' Mess for lunch when the tannoy went and I scrambled after a flying bomb coming in over Rye. It took some catching, as we were only supposed to keep the Merlin's over boost revs on for less than ten minutes or it meant an engine change. I soon saw it and opened fire, but I was too precise and enthusiastic – I never got such a shock in the air as when I hit it. The V1 went up with a terrific explosion – this first one blew up in front of me. My God! I never thought the aircraft would stand the shock, or the debris that hit it, and the left wing flew off above me. When I got back my wingtips had to be changed.'

Murkowski destroyed another the next day, while on the 5th WO Czeslaw Barllomiejczyk shot down a flying bomb off Folkstone – the first success by a future Mustang III V1 ace. Many others would set out on a similar path over the next week or so.

To reinforce the campaign against the V1s, on 9 July the Polish wing moved into RAF Brenzett ALG, in Kent, so as to cover the Dover-Folkestone-Rye coastal line up to the London balloon barrage. At around this time No 129 Sqn's CO 'Wag' Haw departed to be replaced by fellow ace Sqn Ldr P D Thompson, and on the 11th the unit's Flg Off James Hartley shot down his first V1 near Folkestone. That same day Flt Sgt Jankowski shot down No 315 Sqn's first V1 at 1310 hrs, while on 12 July No 129 Sqn's seven-victory ace Flt Lt Desmond Ruchwaldy claimed the first of his 8.5 V1s. That same day one of the leading Polish V1 aces, WO Tadeusz Szymanski, claimed two. One of these was downed in a less than conventional way, as he later described;

'The thing was jerking along and the elevator was flapping with each vibration of the cruise jet motor. I noticed there were no ailerons and also

One of the leading Polish V1 aces was WO Tadeusz Szymanski of No 316 Sqn, who is seen here examining the wingtip of his Mustang III after he had tipped up a V1 on 12 July 1944 (*Polish Institute and Sikorski Archive*)

that on the front of the bomb was a silly little propeller. It looked ridiculous. I decided to try to tip the "Doodlebug" up with my wingtip. As soon as I put my port wing under the "Doodlebug's" wing it started lifting. I let it straighten itself out, then I put enough of the front part of my wingtip under its wingtip, taking care to keep my aileron out of the way, and then by banking sharply to starboard I hit it with the port tip. This failed to topple the bomb, so I tried a slightly different manoeuvre, hitting it very hard with my wingtip

Polish pilots examine No 129 Sqn's 'Diver' scoreboard, which was actually part of the wing of a V1 that unit had brought down on 10 July 1944 (*via Wojtek Matusiak*)

as I went up like in a loop. To my dismay the "Doodlebug" was still flying perfectly straight, and then I realised that the engine was now underneath. I had turned it upside down! I could see it was gradually going into a dive, and then down it went.'

However, his squadronmate Flt Sgt Aleksander Pietrzak (in FB378) had fired on one that same day and then been caught in the blast as the V1 exploded. He bailed out safely. Szymanski claimed yet another flying bomb on 6 August.

With the Germans launching hundreds of V1s per day, the defending units were kept busy having to mount standing patrols outside the anti-aircraft gun belts. Individual scores soon mounted, and 23 July saw the emergence of the first Mustang III V1 aces when Flt Sgt Stanislaw Rudowski of No 306 Sqn destroyed his fifth (of nine and two shared), along with Flt Lt Jan Siekierski – one of the unit's flight commanders – who brought down three 'Doodlebugs' over central Kent during the course of the day.

With the enemy able to launch V1s round the clock, the Mustang III flew a handful of trial night flights in an effort to improve the nocturnal defences. Future ace Flt Lt Michal Cwynar of No 315 Sqn recalled;

'We chose a clear, moonless night, thinking it would be easier to detect the "Doodlebugs'" orange-red coloured exhaust flames. In the darkness, without the aircraft's positional lights, Horbaczewski got airborne for a two-hour patrol. After his safe landing, I took off to continue the night patrol. We did not intercept any flying bombs, and that was the end of the night flights.'

Shortly afterwards No 96 Sqn, equipped with Mosquito nightfighters at nearby RAF Ford, in Sussex, used a Mustang III for more anti-V1 trials. Amongst the pilots to fly it was the unit CO, nightfighter ace Wg Cdr Edward Crew, albeit without success. The Mustang III units continued to claim heavily by day, however, with No 129 Sqn's Flg Off James Hartley (in HB862) bringing down two near Folkestone on 7 August to become a V1 ace.

As the 'Diver' threat waned, the squadrons gradually began flying occasional escort missions, as well as supporting the breakout from Normandy. The last V1s claimed by Mustang IIIs during the summer assault on England were appropriately shot down by No 129 Sqn pilots on 29 August. Desmond Ruchwaldy destroyed his ninth over the sea to the east of Dungeness, while another V1 ace, Flt Lt Tony Osborne (in FB392) shot down his sixth and Flg Off James Hartley (in FB138) got his twelfth south of Folkstone – the latter kill made Hartley the most successful Mustang III pilot against the V1 menace.

WITH THE USAAF

It became quickly apparent that the USAAF strategy of a daylight bombing campaign against Germany was dependent on the provision of suitable fighter escort, to which the P-51 was to prove so successful. However, for much of 1943 the only American fighter types available to perform this mission were the twin-engined P-38 Lightning and the massive P-47 Thunderbolt, both of which were widely used.

With strong US-Polish connections established through immigration to America, a number of Poles serving with the RAF's Polish squadrons obtained attachment to USAAF fighter units based in England. The most successful of these was undoubtedly Flt Lt 'Mike' Gladych who, having become an ace flying Spitfires in early 1944, obtained a posting to the 56th FG's 61st FS, flying P-47Ds, and achieved a further ten victories. Another Pole to achieve success with this squadron was Flt Lt Witold Lanowski, who gained four victories, while Flg Off Tadeusz Andersz, who was also with the 61st FS, shot down a Bf 109 southeast of Kiel on 9 February 1944 – he later returned to the RAF to command No 315 Sqn. Other Poles serving with P-51 units during early 1944 included nine victory ace Flt Lt 'Toni' Glowacki, who flew with the 354th FG's 356th FS. The full story of these pilots' exploits in the USAAF is detailed in *Osprey Aircraft of the Aces 21 – Polish Aces of World War 2.*

The expansion of the Eighth Air Force's VIII Fighter Command also led to the attachment of some RAF pilots so that they could gain experience of long-range fighter operations. Among them was ten-victory ace Wg Cdr Peter Wickham, who joined the 4th FG at Debden, in Essex, while Flt Lt Jack Cleland became the only RNZAF fighter pilot to fly with the Eighth Air Force when he joined the 357th FG's 363rd FS at Leiston, in Suffolk, on 5 July. Having claimed two victories flying Spitfire VIIs with No 616 Sqn on 12 June 1944, he made his first flight in a P-51 on 15 July – Cleland was allocated his own aircraft, P-51D 44-13573/B6-V, on the 21st.

Also seconded during the summer of 1944 was Flt Lt Warren Peglar of the RCAF, who recalled for the author;

'I was given the option of either going to a training station in northern England, where I would be instructing new pilots in fighter escort combat techniques, or being posted to the Eighth Air Force and get experience on P-51 Mustangs. The RAF was interested in commencing daylight heavy bombing, and to do this it would need experienced personnel to staff long-range fighter wings. I jumped at the chance, and was posted to the 355th FG's 354th FS, based at Steeple Morden, some 40 miles north of London. I arrived on 12 July 1944 and stayed there until 25 September, when I flew my last combat trip with the Yanks. I then returned to the RAF and rejoined my old squadron.'

Peglar was soon operational, and on 3 August he flew his fifth mission in P-51D WR-Q, as the 354th FS mission summary recorded;

'Escorted at 21-22,000 ft until squadron bounced by 10+ Me 109s at approximately 1515 hrs, 10 miles southeast of Mannheim. Squadron approaching southbound bombers from "three o'clock". Approximately 10-12 enemy aircraft bounced from "seven o'clock high". In ensuing combat, squadron split up and Flt Lt Peglar (RCAF) and Capt Lenfest each destroyed a Me-109. As one flight approached bombers from "two o'clock" to resume escort six Me-109s and Fw 190s observed making stern attack on bombers. Flight turned and engaged enemy aircraft, Flt Lt Peglar destroying an Fw 190.'

Three days later on 6 August, the Eighth Air Force targeted Danzig, and among the escorting pilots were Cleland, Peglar and RAF pilot Flt Lt Eric Woolley, who was flying with the 357th FG's 362nd FS. This was one of the famous Shuttle Missions that continued east to land at Piryatin, in Ukraine, after 6 hours 45 minutes in the air. The following day they escorted the B-17s from Ukraine to targets in southeast Poland, before returning to Piryatin.

Flt Lt Warren Peglar (on wing) discusses the relative merits of the Spitfire and P-51 with his CO in the 354th FS, seven-victory ace Maj Bert Marshall. Peglar was credited with four victories plus one strafing kill during his attachment to the Eighth Air Force in the summer of 1944 (*W R Peglar*)

On the 8th the B-17s struck Ploesti, in Rumania, before landing at San Severo. A few days later the American fighters escorted more B-17s from Italy to southwest France, before the Mustangs returned to England after seven-and-a-half hours in the air.

Going down to strafe the airfield at Dole/Tavaux, close to the Swiss border, Warren Peglar destroyed a Ju 52/3m just as it landed, so claiming a 'ground kill'. He continued to fly regular long-range escorts to Eighth Air Force raids through into September, and on the 11th he was flying P-51D 'WR-S' south of Kassell, as he recalled to the author specifically for this volume;

'I was at "eight o'clock" to a box of B-24s at 24,000 ft. As I looked over, a gaggle of at least six Me 109s hit them, and I saw one B-24 catch fire. I dropped my wing tanks, peeled off to the right and went after a Me 109 some 2000 ft below me. I had to do a tight diving turn to get behind him, and as I pulled into position the pilot bailed out without me firing a shot!

'Five minutes later I spotted another fighter, and diving on it I closed in and opened fire, seeing hits on the wing root and fuselage. The Me 109 immediately began to stream smoke and pieces fell off, but the Hun pilot went into a very skilled display of low-level flying, combined with good evasive skidding and slipping. I finally got fed up with this and closed to about 50 yards and waited for him to straighten out. He did, and I let

One of the Mustangs flown by
Flt Lt Warren Peglar during his
secondment to the 355th FG's 354th
FS at Steeple Morden was P-51B
42-106950/WR-P *The Iowa Beaut*.
His first operation in it was
escorting 1300 bombers to Munich
on 31 July 1944 and his last was
an escort to Berlin on 27 August
(*W R Peglar*)

him have about a six-second burst and got strikes on the wings and
cockpit area. Then the canopy came off, as did pieces of the Me 109.
He pulled up to approximately 50 ft and bailed out over a town, though
the 'chute failed to open.'

At this time the Eighth Air Force recognised 'ground' kills, and so Warren
Peglar duly became the only seconded pilot to become an ace (albeit
in Eighth Air Force terms). Also claiming on this mission was
Flt Lt Lionel Frost, who was assigned to the 357th FG's 358th FS at
Leiston. He was credited with one Bf 109 destroyed and a second one
damaged in the air, plus several more on the ground. Warren Peglar's last
mission was on 25 September, flying in the lead flight on the last Shuttle
Mission (codenamed *Frantic VII*) over Warsaw.

One of the last secondments to the Eighth Air Force was made by the
Belgian ace Flt Lt Andre Plisnier, who flew P-51s with the 4th FG's 336th
FS between November 1944 and January 1945. He was unable to add
to his score of three and three shared destroyed, however.

BREAKOUT FROM NORMANDY

Although the Mustangs of No 133 Wing had been diverted to the V1
campaign, the squadrons of No 122 Wing continued to support the
heavy fighting in Normandy that was to lead to the eventual breakout and
rout of the Wehrmacht in France. Among the most important duties for
Allied air power in addition to protecting ground forces from air attack
was to ensure that bridges over the River Seine were permanently
disabled, thus preventing German mechanised troops from escaping. The
Luftwaffe countered when able, mounting more than 500 sorties on
5 July for example.

In late June 1944 No 122 Sqn moved across to the ALG at B7 Martragny, in France, where FZ114/MT-A is seen being prepared for a mission among the wheat fields. Ranking RAF Mustang III ace Flt Lt Maurice Pinches made most of his claims when flying this aircraft, including on 15 July when he shared in the destruction of a Ju 188 to 'make ace' (*P H T Green collection*)

That afternoon No 122 Sqn flew another armed reconnaissance to the northwest of Paris, where a solitary Bf 109 was found and shot down. The first to attack was Flg Off 'Jimmy' Talalla (in FB180), who had chased the Messerschmitt in and out of cloud before having a very close encounter;

'On coming out of cloud I found myself one wing span away on the starboard side of the Me 109. The Hun pilot looked me in the face before breaking away to port, and then to starboard. I got a short burst in.'

Flt Lt Allan Pavey (in FZ167) then fired, before Flg Off A W Minchin (in FZ177) attacked the Bf 109 and it blew up – this was Pavey's fifth victory on Mustang IIIs.

The omnipresent Allied fighters were now having a real effect, and such support that the Luftwaffe could give to its embattled comrades on the ground was, perforce, extremely limited.

On 8 July a patrol from No 19 Sqn, led by Flt Lt Deryck Lamb (in FB113), was the only one to meet any opposition. Flying over the Caen-Villers Bocage area, they spotted a pair of Bf 109s that were both shot down. The two shared victories took Lamb to acedom. It was an appropriate swansong, for the following day he was promoted and given command of No 65 Sqn. A few days later, on 12 July, Lamb's erstwhile CO, 'Mac' Gilmour (in FB201), led a patrol that encountered more than a dozen Bf 109s from JG 1 south of Caen, and he shot one of them down for his ninth, and final, victory. On the evening of 15 July, Maurice Pinches (in FZ114) also achieved acedom when his section shot down Ju 88A-4 L1+BN of 4./KG 6, flown by Feldwebel Günther Parge;

'I fired at 500 yards, closing to 150 yards dead astern, and saw strikes on the fuselage, port wing and engine. I then watched Flg Offs Tickner (in FZ106) and Hargreaves (in FB232) conclude the destruction.'

The Ju 88 force-landed at Thornery.

Early morning mists were now affecting some operations, but with Caen finally falling, fighting to break the German front before the Seine now began in earnest. As ever, it was ground fire that caused the most losses to 2nd TAF aircraft. No 122 Wing moved a little further forward to B12 Ellon and B24 St Andre de l'Eure in the middle of the month, before quickly resuming operations. It supported ill-fated Operation *Goodwood*, which commenced on 18 July and suffered heavy losses in tanks against a well prepared foe. Rain then turned both the battlefield and the ALGs into quagmires, greatly interfering with operations. Nevertheless, this command of the air led Generalfeldmarschall Günther von Kluge, the Wehrmacht's Commander-in-Chief West, to conclude 'there is no possibility of our finding a strategy which will counter-balance its truly annihilating effect unless we give up the field of battle'.

The breakout battle finally began in the American sector on 25 July, and with improved weather the fighters were out in force. Shortly before midday Wg Cdr Johnston led elements of Nos 65 and 122 Sqns on an armed reconnaissance into the Falaise area, where they bombed marshalling yards before being intercepted by 40+ enemy fighters. In the ensuing battle he shared in the destruction of an Fw 190 to record his final victory. No 65 Sqn downed several Bf 109s too, with the one claimed by Flt Sgt 'Ned' Kelly (in FZ125) being the unit's 100th kill, and his fourth.

The following evening it was No 122 Sqn's opportunity to 'get stuck in' when its pilots encountered 30+ enemy fighters, probably from I. and II./JG 2, around Laigle. No fewer than six Fw 190s were claimed shot down, and four others damaged. Flt Lt Allan Pavey (in FZ167) shot down one, probably destroyed a second and damaged three more, while American Plt Off Jim Thorne (in FB180) downed two to become an ace in dramatic fashion, as he later described;

'Diving slightly and opening up, I pulled away from the squadron and thus contacted the enemy aircraft first. Picking the stbd aircraft in the smaller formation, I opened fire from 500 yards. I saw strikes on his starboard wing, but then had to break as eight Huns were behind me. One dived down in front of me and I got onto his tail. He broke to port and I followed. At 400 yards I fired short bursts, observing strikes on his tail unit. He half rolled and dived vertically downwards. Following him in a steep diving turn, I saw him dive straight into the ground.

'Simultaneously three FW 190s that were above dived on me and I was hit in the starboard flap. The four of us began to mill around firing. Eventually, at 7000 ft I picked another enemy aircraft which flew across in front of me. He dived to starboard and then zoomed upwards. Following, I caught him easily on the zoom, and closing to 75 yards I opened fire as he almost stalled. He attempted to half roll, and in doing so I got many strikes along the length of his aircraft. Pieces flew off and he dived vertically. Following him down in a tight spiral, I saw him hit the ground when I was at 4000 ft.'

Thorne then rejoined and set course for base, but engine trouble resulted in him force-landing on a strip at St Aubin.

There was further action for No 122 Sqn the following morning when Maurice Pinches (in FB164) destroyed an Fw 190 near Pont L'Eveque and shared another with Flg Off R E Tickner (in FB232). Although these were his final claims, they were to make Pinches the RAF's most

successful Mustang III pilot with five and three shared victories. Sadly, however, in this same action his fellow ace Flt Lt Allan Pavey (in FZ167) was shot down and killed.

On 29 July it was No 65 Sqn's turn to encounter the enemy, with Sqn Ldr Deryck Lamb (in FB186) claiming his fifth on the Mustang III near Evreux;

'I found myself with two '109s on my tail. These turned so tightly as to force me to spin down into cloud at 3000 ft. I climbed back up, and on breaking cloud I found a '109 with a jettison tank on about to enter thin cloud. I closed in on him and opened fire as he entered cloud and picked him up underneath, giving him another three-second burst from 300 yards. I went through and picked him up on top of the cloud, this time closing, and I opened fire with a four-second burst and saw strikes on the fuselage, wing root and tail on the port side. The '109 emitted thick brown smoke and went into cloud again. I followed him and found him under cloud still pouring smoke, and as I closed in to finish him off he broke right tightly, streaming white smoke from the wing tips. After turning 90 degrees, he suddenly flicked over onto his back and spun in, still complete with jet tank, exploding as he hit the ground about a mile north of Evreux.'

FALAISE POCKET

Back in England, although being committed to countering the V1, the squadrons of No 133 Wing were also tasked with some escort sorties, the most successful of which was flown on 30 July. That day Mustang IIIs from No 315 Sqn led by Sqn Ldr Horbaczewski (in FB166) flew up to RAF Coltishall, where they refuelled, and after lunch set out to escort an anti-shipping sweep by Beaufighters off the southwest coast of Norway. Flying close to their charges, as they approached the coast the weather

No 315 Sqn's charismatic CO was Sqn Ldr Eugeniusz Horbaczewski, and he flew FB382/PK-G which was decorated with his unit's badge and his impressive score. Here, the groundcrew pose for a snapshot with the fighter at RAF Coolham ALG after having fitted it with two 500-lb bombs (*Dr J P Koniarek archive via Wojtek Matusiak*)

cleared into bright sunshine, and off Lista Bf 109s of 11. and 12./JG 5 were sighted preparing to attack the Beaufighters. Horbaczewski led his section against the inner group of German fighters, while Flt Lt Michal Cwynar's went for the others, as the latter recalled many years later;

'In diving and climbing in a left hard turn, I engaged the group leader. By the way in which he scythed through the air, the edges of his "Messer's" wings stitching the sky with air-condensed threads, I realised that he was a good pilot. He pulled out hard, but so did I! I lowered flaps ten degrees and was gaining on him. I got him in my gunsight's illuminated ring, pulled straight through his line of flight, one diameter, two, three of deflection, and then pressed the firing button. For a split second there was nothing, then I saw the bullets punching holes first in his tail section and then the fuselage, canopy and wings.'

This victory took him to acedom. Cwynar's CO also bagged another Bf 109, reporting afterwards, 'I dived down on them and gave one a three-second burst, after which he caught fire and went straight into the sea'. He shared a second, as did Cwynar, in a haul of eight destroyed for no loss. They returned in good spirits to England, making landfall in Yorkshire.

In Normandy the enemy was now in the throes of withdrawing into what became the Falaise Pocket, and river traffic was a key target for the fighter-bombers. No 19 Sqn had a number of successes, including on 8 August when its new CO, Sqn Ldr Bill Loud (in FB366) claimed a Bf 109 for his third victory and, in the same action near Chartres, Flt Sgt Basilios Vassiliades (in FB116) scored his final kill on the Mustang III;

'I spotted two Me109s at "six o'clock" about 500 yards behind me. I turned and engaged one, finishing my turn about 400 yards behind him. With my third burst I saw several hits on the cockpit, apparently killing the pilot because the enemy aircraft immediately went into a shallow dive, striking the ground and completely disintegrating.'

Late the next day, during an attack on the Seine barges, the squadron found some Fw190s and four were shot down. 'Buck' Collyns (in FB116) outlined his elevation to acedom in his report;

'I dived down with my section and intercepted one Fw 190 which had turned and was flying west. I attacked at ground level, firing a burst from a range of 300 yards, and the aircraft pulled up and stall turned. I fired a second burst whilst he was turning and saw strikes. Following him

No 133 Wing was led during the summer of 1944 by Polish ace Grp Capt Tadeusz Nowierski, who was allocated Mustang HB886 as his personal mount. Bearing his initials, the fighter was being flown by him during a 'Ramrod' on 5 August when he shot down a V1 flying bomb near Arnhem that had been launched in the direction of the Belgian port of Antwerp (*Polish Institute and Sikorski Archive*)

round and still firing, I saw more strikes. The Fw 190 then pulled up into a stall turn for a second time, and I got in a good burst at 75 yards, seeing him turn onto his back, hit the ground and explode.'

Collyns also shared in the destruction of another Fw 190 with WO S J Larsen (in FX887). Ground fire was the undoing of Vassiliades (in FB116) on his last Mustang III trip on 11 August, as he ruefully noted in his logbook following his return. 'Shot down by flak at 1215 hrs over Elbeuf. Caught fire and bailed out at 500 ft. Evaded capture and returned to No 122 Wing on the 28th'. The previous day Maurice Pinches (in FX951) had been shot down in error by USAAF P-38s while air testing a Mustang III, the ace bailing out with slight burns.

The Poles of Nos 306 and 315 Sqn also occasionally operated over Normandy during this period, having been released from V1 duties. Early on the 18th – the day when the mouth of the Falaise Pocket had all but been closed – Horbaczewski (in FB355) led a dozen Mustang IIIs from No 315 Sqn to Beauvais, where they caught elements of II./JG 2 forming up. In next to no time the Poles had claimed to have shot down 16 Fw 190s, although in fact ten fell. Among those who claimed was Flt Sgt Jakub Bargielowski, who shot down two and damaged two more, while his flight commander Flt Lt Henryk Pietrzak shot down two more and shared a third near the airfield. No 315 suffered only one loss, but it was that of its mercurial CO, Horbaczewski, who was seen to shoot down three to take his score to 16.5 kills prior to his demise. It was a severe loss.

The intensity of the air fighting continued over the Falaise Pocket as the remnants of the German 7th Army attempted to escape from encirclement and destruction. Mid-morning on 19 August saw No 19 Sqn engaging in strafing the retreating enemy when a substantial force of fighters was spotted. The German aircraft quickly withdrew, but not before the youthful WO Max Bell (in FX887) had claimed his coveted fifth success;

'We broke to port and I selected an FW 190 that went into a steep climbing turn to port. I fired a two second burst from 200 yards, closing to 130 yards. With this burst I observed strikes on the starboard wing, and with a second burst of three seconds saw strikes on the cockpit, which burst into flames and the hood flew off. The enemy aircraft spiral dived in flames and I saw it crash and burn on the deck.'

Mustang III FB226/MT-K of No 122 Sqn was the usual aircraft of Flg Off E A Roemmele, but it was also occasionally flown by ace Flg Off 'Jimmy' Talalla through the summer in ground attacks on the retreating Wehrmacht (*E A Roemmele via R L Ward*)

The following evening, during a sweep over Paris at 2000 hrs, Flt Lt Lance Burra-Robinson claimed three during a wing sweep to become an ace in spectacular fashion. His CO, Sqn Ldr Lamb, however, had a torrid time with these Fw 190s from I./JG 11, but managed to extricate himself and claim one shot down with another pilot. No 19 Sqn's 'Buck' Collyns (in FB194) was seen to destroy another before he was killed. A sweepstake had been running as to who would claim the wing's 122nd victory, but the nine kills claimed on this date complicated the matter, so the names of the successful pilots went into a hat and the honour given to No 19 Sqn's Flt Sgt W G Abbott (in FZ140).

The great pursuit of the shattered Wehrmacht then commenced with incredible speed, the enemy being constantly harried by Allied fighter-bombers. The squadrons of No 122 Wing moved several times during this period, and by early September they were located at B60 Grimbergen, to the north of Brussels, from where they continued operations. 9 September was a black day, however, for at 1345 hrs both WO Bell (FX887) and Flt Sgt Abbot (in FB148) were shot down by flak while attacking trains near Apeldoorn. The latter was killed but the unfortunate Bell was captured by Dutch collaborators and handed over to the SS, who shot him out of hand.

Later that same afternoon No 65 Sqn's CO, Sqn Ldr Deryck Lamb (in FB129) was shot down near Zwolle-Lengahm and bailed out injured. In spite of being shot at whilst hanging beneath his parachute, Lamb managed to evade capture and, linking up with the Resistance, returned to Allied lines ten days later – Lance Burra-Robinson was promoted to replace him. The deadly flak claimed another ace the following day too when Plt Off Jim Thorne (in FB372) of No 122 Sqn was killed over Velp, the wreckage of his aircraft hitting the town and killing several civilians.

On 17 September No 122 Wing mounted standing patrols over the Nijmegen area covering the Allied airborne landings in Holland – Operation *Market Garden*, which drew an immediate enemy response. No 65 Sqn lost two Mustangs to flak, but also saw the first enemy fighters for some days, claiming one destroyed, as did No 19 Sqn a little later, although it too lost two aircraft. Intense air operations continued to support the increasingly beleaguered 'Paras' trapped in Arnhem, and over Nijmegen on the 25th No 122 Sqn's Flt Lt 'Jimmy' Talalla (in FB187) reached acedom;

'Closing to 300 yards, I opened fire. The Hun was extremely low at the time, and after a two-second burst I saw strikes on the engine and fuselage. I broke off my attack for a moment, and before I could resume the enemy aircraft hit the ground.'

Two more fighters were claimed by the squadron in this fight. The Poles too were active, as near Arnhem Henryk Pietrzak of No 315 Sqn made his final claim when he shared an Fw 190 – this claim made him a Mustang III ace. Flying his personal aircraft HB866/JZ, the No 133 Wing leader Wg Cdr Jan Zumbach probably destroyed a Bf 109 in the same area to register his last claim too. That day also No 306 Sqn's CO, Sqn Ldr Pawel Niemiec, was replaced by the veteran Sqn Ldr Josef Zulikowski, who was to lead the unit for the rest of the war.

A few days later the three Mustang III squadrons of No 122 Wing were withdrawn back to England for long-range escort duties.

Malayan born but of Singhalese extraction, Flg Off 'Jimmy' Talalla's third Mustang III victory near Nijmegen on 25 September took him to acedom. He had previously claimed one and one shared destroyed flying Spitfire VBs with No 118 Sqn in 1943 (*via C F Shores*)

LONG-RANGE ESCORT

By the early autumn of 1944 Bomber Command 'heavies' were regularly flying daylight raids against targets in the western part of Germany, and the three Mustang III squadrons on the Continent – Nos 19, 65 and 122 – had been transferred to Air Defence of Great Britain (as Fighter Command was then designated) control in order to perform the long-range escort task to which they were ideally suited. In late September the units moved to RAF Matlaske, in Norfolk but in mid-October they settled in at RAF Andrews Field, in Essex, where they joined the three squadrons from No 133 Wing – Nos 129, 306 and 315 – and No 316 Sqn to form a seven squadron 'super wing'.

Other units were re-equipping with the American fighter too so as to enable the escort task to be fully supported. The first Mustang III arrived at RAF North Weald, also in Essex, as a replacement for No 234 Sqn's by now thoroughly obsolete Spitfire VBs on 29 September, along with '36 screwdrivers of a special kind necessary to maintain it'! Conversion to the new aircraft was speedy, with the squadron flying 28 familiarisation sorties on the 30th alone. Of particular significance was the fact that pilots noted its great range with external tanks, which would clearly allow penetrations with heavy bombers deep into Germany.

Gunnery training began on 2 October, and No 234 Sqn was declared operational on the 12th. Its experience was typical for other units that would convert from Spitfires to Mustang III/IVs in coming months.

In spite of escorting daylight raids for the rest of the war, the opportunities presented to the RAF's escort force for aerial combat were to be far more limited than those enjoyed by their USAAF equivalents. This was primarily because the RAF raids usually did not penetrate as deep into Germany, and were less frequent, so as a consequence the numbers of claims, though significant, were more modest.

Some of No 19 Sqn's Mustang IIIs are serviced soon after arriving at RAF Matlaske for escort duties in late September 1944. The nearest one is FB142/QV-F, which was regularly flown by future ace Flt Lt Peter Hearne later in the year and into early 1945 (*No 19 Sqn Records*)

Flt Lt Henryk Pietrzak included four and two shared victories on the Mustang III in his overall tally. He is seen here relaxing against KH574/WC-A of No 309 Sqn, which was the regular mount of his CO, and fellow ace, Sqn Ldr 'Toni' Glowacki (*Pietrzak family*)

No 65 Sqn became operational from Matlaske almost immediately, flying its first escort to a raid by 120 Halifaxes on Bergen, in Norway. Shortly afterwards the Poles began operations from Andrews Field, with No 315 Sqn (led by Henryk Pietrzak) mounting a 'Ramrod' over the Achmer-Paderborn. Seeing little air activity, they subsequently strafed ground targets, although one aircraft had to make an emergency landing near Eindhoven. A few days later Wg Cdr Zumbach led another mission escorting a Lancaster raid. The three Matlaske squadrons moved across to Andrews Field on 14 October, but without their most successful pilot. Maurice Pinches had suddenly contracted jaundice and in spite of urgent medical care he died in hospital at the end of the month. This was a particularly tragic end for the RAF's most successful Mustang III pilot.

By October No 309 Sqn, based at RAF Drem in East Lothian, was also converting to the Mustang III. Led by 8.5-victory ace Sqn Ldr 'Toni' Glowacki, who had gained experience with the USAAF earlier in the year, the unit would also move down to Andrews Field in December.

Meanwhile, No 234 Sqn had begun operations from North Weald by covering some pathfinder Mosquitos that had been to Duisberg on 14 October and a raid by 128 Lancasters on Bonn four days later. That same day the Poles had been in action over Denmark and northeast of Aalborg, Flt Lt Janusz Walawski (in HB855) of No 316 Sqn shooting down a pair of Bf 109s for the first of four kills that he would claim with the Mustang III. As this mission clearly proved, there was a need for long-range escort fighters to support the coastal strike wings, so by the end of the month No 315 Sqn had been moved to RAF Peterhead, in Aberdeenshire, although it would re-join the Andrews Field Wing in mid-January 1945.

As the autumn deepened and the days shortened, the wing at Andrews Field began to increase the pace of its operations, with some elements providing close escort while others flew supporting sweeps. Like their Eighth Air Force brethren, once their charges were safely en-route home, and if fuel permitted, the squadrons would sweep known areas of enemy activity. A typical mission from this period was flown by North Weald-based No 234 Sqn at the end of October when the unit gave target cover to a Lancaster attack and flew a sweep over Frankfurt. No 65 Sqn also embraced the 'freelancing' aspect of the bomber escort business during the early afternoon of 2 November when its CO, Sqn Ldr Lance Burra-Robinson, led a 'Rodeo' from Andrews Field to northwest Germany in support of a raid by 184 Lancasters on Homberg. Two hours later, when west of Minden at 8000 ft, four Fw 190s were spotted. Flt Lt Peter Hearne subsequently recalled;

'I saw four aircraft at "11 o'clock" on a reciprocal course below us. At first I thought they were Tempests, as we had previously seen them in the area, but as they passed below us I recognised them as Fw 190s and then broke to port through 180 degrees, chasing after the enemy aircraft. I selected the nearest and got into position about 250 yards astern. The Fw 190 pulled up, then dived in steep spiral turns to about 2000 ft, when it pulled up in a steep starboard turn, losing speed. I was able to turn inside and fire a two-second burst from a range of 200 yards. I saw strikes behind and below the cockpit, and the aircraft dived for the ground in a westerly direction. I followed about 450 yards astern expecting it to crash, as it was pouring white smoke. After about two minutes the aircraft pulled up in a steep climbing turn to port, and again I was able to turn inside it and fire another one-and-a-half-second burst from about 200 yards. The aircraft was then "up sun", and I did not see any strikes, but the hood came away and the Fw 190 turned onto its back, stalled and dived into the ground, whereupon it exploded, about 20 miles east of Minden.'

This was the first of Hearne's five kills, and the Mustang IIIs landed back at base shortly after 1700 hrs, although Flt Sgt Shannon was posted missing.

These lengthy missions were fairly typical fare for the seven Mustang III squadrons based in eastern England through the latter weeks of 1944. Operations by the Andrews Field Wing continued, and on 12 December – the day after Wg Cdr Kamirez Rutowski had taken over as the wing

The wing and squadron commanders of the Bentwaters Wing, several of them established aces, gather for a photograph in early 1945. Even though the conflict in Europe was in its final stage, sadly, not all of these men would survive the war. They are, from left to right, Sqn Ldr Tony Drew (CO of No 118 Sqn), Sqn Ldr Barry Gale (CO of No 165 Sqn), Sqn Ldr Peter Thompson (CO of No 129 Sqn), Wg Cdr Johnny Plagis (Bentwaters Wing leader), Wg Cdr Mike Donnet (Andrews Field wing leader), Sqn Ldr 'Jas' Storrar (No 234 Sqn CO), Sqn Ldr R E Green (No 64 Sqn CO) and Maj Arne Austeen (No 126 Sqn CO) (ww2images)

Leader of the Bentwaters Wing when first formed was Wg Cdr Harold Bird-Wilson, who had the gauntlet badge of his old Battle of Britain unit, No 17 Sqn, painted on the tail of his personal Mustang III KH500/HBW (*HAC Bird-Wilson via C F Shores*)

Leader – no fewer than 88 Mustangs escorted 140 Lancasters against a steelworks at Witten. The bombers were attacked from above by around 50 Bf 109s that were in turn engaged by the escorting fighters, which claimed five destroyed. One fell to Flt Lt Dale Stephens (in FX954) of No 122 Sqn over Dortmund – this was his second Mustang III victory. Another was claimed by new No 19 Sqn CO Peter Hearne, who was also credited with a probable and a damaged.

Flying FZ194/SZ-V, No 316 Sqn's Flt Lt Janusz Walawski claimed his fourth victory, but frustratingly, his all-important fifth never came – although he did subsequently destroy two aircraft on the ground on 19 April 1945. One of the Mustang IIIs was shot down, however, as were no fewer than eight Lancasters.

Two days later No 309 Sqn was posted in to Andrews Field from Scotland, thus bringing the wing back up to strength. The newcomers began operations soon afterwards.

THE NEW WING

The Mustang III had quickly proven itself to be far better suited to the long-range escort role than the Spitfire IXs that were also in use at the time, and this resulted in the formation of a second 'large' wing at RAF Bentwaters, in Suffolk, under the experienced leadership of ace Wg Cdr Harold Bird-Wilson. Thus in mid-December Sqn Ldr Peter Thompson's No 129 Sqn finally left No 133 Wing and joined the new Bentwaters Wing, as did No 234 Sqn. They were joined at the end of the month by No 64 Sqn under Sqn Ldr Cliff Rudland (who had several victories from his time flying Whirlwind Is with No 263 Sqn in 1941), and No 126 Sqn, then led by Rhodesian Malta ace Sqn Ldr Johnny Plagis, though he was later promoted to become the wing leader. Both these units had previously been flying Spitfire IXs in the bomber escort role.

Conditions at the new base were bleak, and although operational facilities were adequate, much of the domestic accommodation took the form of huts surrounded by a veritable sea of mud! The wing gained a formidable new squadron commander too when, on 21 December, Norwegian ace Maj Werner Christie was posted in from HQ No 11 Group at RAF Bentley Priory, in Middlesex, to command No 234 Sqn. He thus became only the second Norwegian to command an RAF unit,

This Mustang III of No 234 Sqn, adorned with rare, and colourful, artwork is thought to be FZ160/AZ-Q. If indeed this is the case, the fighter was taken up on a familiarisation by the unit's new CO, Maj Werner Christie, on the day he joined the unit in December 1944. On 3 January 1945 it was flown by another successful pilot in the form of Flt Lt Peter Steib during an escort for RAF bombers sent to attack oil installations at Castrup (*via Norman Franks*)

and was airborne that day on a familiarisation and air test in FZ160/AZ-Q. The wing became operational two days later when it escorted a raid on Trier by 150+ Lancasters, Flt Lt James Butler (in FX972) of No 65 Sqn bagging an Fw 190 over Cologne for his first victory.

On 24 December Werner Christie led the top cover to 160 Lancasters and Halifaxes attacking Dusseldorf, where very heavy flak was noted in the target area. There was little let up over the festive season, with Christie leading his squadron on the 28th in an escort for 150 Lancasters targeting Cologne, and the next day Koblenz was attacked by 200 bombers, again escorted by Bentwaters Wing Mustang IIIs. By this time No 165 Sqn, commanded by 14-victory ace Sqn Ldr 'Jas' Storrar, had also arrived at Bentwaters, and it began converting to the Mustang III in January.

On New Year's Day 1945 the Andrews Field squadrons were up once more, Nos 309 and 316 providing cover for a morning attack on Landsbergen, while in the afternoon wing leader Wg Cdr Bill Loud led others to Munchen-Gladbach. The following day Nos 309 and 316 Sqns mounted an ultimately uneventful 'Ramrod' to the Lake Lascher-Lipstadt area. V1 ace Flt Lt Teofil Szymankiewicz of No 316 Sqn crash-landed in Belgium, however, and later died from the injuries he sustained. The wing was up on 3 January too helping escort a raid on Dortmund, and although a Mustang III was hit by flak it landed in Belgium.

At Bentwaters that day No 126 Sqn began operations, covering Lancasters bombing Dortmund – Werner Christie, flying FX124/AZ-N, led No 234 Sqn on the same operation. Bird-Wilson, flying a No 64 Sqn aircraft, headed up the wing on the 5th, Flt Lt Ray Stebbings of No 234 Sqn noting in his logbook, 'Escort 150 Lancs Ludwigshaven. Huns up, No 129 Sqn got 2 ME 109s'. One of these fell to Flt Lt Dennis Parker (in FX983) for his second, and final, victory. Such missions were the daily fare, though the bitter winter weather often intervened – Nos 19, 65 and 122 Sqns, led by Wg Cdr Loud, were delayed on the 11th due to a severe snowstorm and had to divert to RAF Manston, in Kent, on their return.

Saarbrucken was the target on the 14th, when both wings participated in the operation, and in the clear weather there were several successful combats. One was fought by the promising 22-year-old Flt Lt David Drew of No 64 Sqn, who described how he shared in two victories near Hochst Oberau airfield in his Combat Report;

'"Silver 2" reported an aircraft at "four o'clock". I ordered tanks to be jettisoned and we dived to attack. It was a Ju 88 at 2000 ft, flying

One of No 118 Sqn's flight commanders was Flt Lt Mike Giddings, who had become an ace the previous year, and whose final claim was made during an escort on 23 March 1945 when he damaged an Me 262 (*W Crutchley*)

into the sun. I gave two bursts and saw strikes. It turned to port and my No 2 gave it a few bursts, setting it on fire. The aircraft crashed in flames on the northern perimeter of Dudelsheim. Return fire was experienced from two guns in the mid-upper position.

'We reformed and set course for Friedburg. After two minutes four aircraft were reported at "two o'clock". We chased these on a northeasterly course and caught up with them over a wood west of Echzell. They were FW 190s. "Gold 3" attacked the starboard one and I took the next on its left. They turned to port and climbed hard, but I held mine and gave it a few bursts, seeing strikes and brown smoke. I then saw "Gold 3's" dive straight into the wood and blow up. "Gold 3" had broken off as my FW 190 was on his tail. I ran out of ammunition but my No 2 gave my FW 190 a burst, and to the accompaniment of its own flak, the aircraft crashed into a wood north of Reichelsheim.'

'Gold 3' was Canadian Flt Lt Don Smiley (in KH430), who also shot down a Bf 109 to register his only victories. During the following day's mission two of No 234 Sqn's aircraft collided over Nijmegen, Flt Lt Stebbings ruefully writing in his logbook some months later, 'Escort 150 Lancs Landreeveer. 1400 hrs, my Mustang was cut in half from behind seat. Reported missing but spent last months as PoW. I came out on 'chute at about 26,000 ft'.

On 16 January No 65 Sqn moved up to Peterhead, exchanging places with No 315 Sqn. No 19 Sqn also moved north a month later, so leaving Andrews Field as a complete Polish wing. The Polish units were out in force on the 17th when, having seen their charges on their way home, the pilots 'had a field day attacking barges on the Rhine River'.

18 January saw the Bentwaters Wing's Mustang III complement expanded still further when No 118 Sqn began re-equipping. It was led by a very successful pilot in the form of Sqn Ldr P W E 'Nip' Heppell, who usually flew NK-A, while one of his flight commanders was Flt Lt Mike Giddings, who had 4.5 victories to his name. No 118 Sqn's first two Mustang IIIs arrived on the 18th, and the conversion of pilots was soon in full swing. By the 21st six more fighters had been delivered, and this number had increased to 18 come early February. By then No 165 Sqn was also operational with the Mustang III, having flown its first mission on 29 January. With No 118 Sqn coming on line a short while later, the Bentwaters Wing was now up to full strength.

Bad weather was now considerably hindering operations, with fog precluding any flying at all on some days towards the end of January. However, on 1 February both wings supported an attack on Munchen-Gladbach that proved uneventful, and was in part preparatory to the advance through the Reichwald Forest and on to the Rhine.

COASTAL ESCORTS

The strike squadrons that Coastal Command employed interdicting shipping off the coasts of Occupied Europe had done so largely unescorted, and had suffered significant losses to enemy fighters as a result, especially off the coast of Norway and Denmark. The arrival of the Mustang III meant that the means to redress this deficiency was now available, and it resulted in the transfer of No 315 Sqn to Peterhead, on the northeast coast of Scotland, in November 1944.

One of its early operations came on the 7 November when seven Liberators were escorted to the Norwegian coast. Flt Sgt Ciundziewicki was lost when he went down to strafe a boat.

Beaufighters of the Dallachy Wing and Mosquitos from the Banff Wing were escorted by a dozen Mustang IIIs to Alesund on 7 December, the latter being led by Wg Cdr Rutkowski (in HB886), who was 'guesting'. About ten miles southwest of Gossen Island they clashed with around 15 Fw 190s and Bf 109s, and in a very brief dogfight claimed four of the Messerschmitt fighters shot down. Sadly Flg Off Czerwinski was shot down, but the aircraft responsible was immediately chased by WO Jakub Bargielowski, who opened fire and had the satisfaction of seeing the Messerschmitt break up – it was a red letter day for him, as this victory was his long-awaited fifth kill.

Bargielowski was himself targeted, but Flt Lt Franek Wiza shot the enemy fighter down into Hano Island before turning on another and destroying it too. Rutkowski probably destroyed a Focke-Wulf for his final claim, while WO Idrian saw two Fw 190s collide as he tried to intercept them and was credited with their destruction as well, so taking his total to four, although he never achieved his fifth victory to 'make ace'.

Other enemy fighters, probably belonging to III./JG 5, then went for the twin-engined aircraft, and Flt Lt Konrad Stembrowicz forced two of them to break off their attacks, one of the German machines having obviously been damaged. He too was then hit and had to pull out with damage. WO Bronislaw Czerwinski was also set upon by a *schwarm*, but he managed to shoot one down before beating a hasty retreat. It had been a major engagement, one result of which was that the faster Mosquitos would not fly with the Beaufighters in future.

No 315 Sqn continued in a like vein for the next month when the weather permitted, but in mid-January 1945 the unit swapped places with No 65 Sqn and returned to Essex. The latter unit had already seen some action on coastal escort work, and as dusk was falling on 9 February a dozen of the squadron's Mustang IIIs were covering a Beaufighter strike in Forde Fjord when a similar number of enemy fighters attacked, two of which were destroyed. One Fw 190 fell to the guns of Flt Lt Jimmy Butler (in KH484) off Kristiansand, his victim almost certainly being 70-victory *experte* Leutnant Rudi Linz. The other fighter fell to Flg Off William Black (in HB836) for his first confirmed, and two more were damaged, one of which was claimed by Flt Lt Johnny Foster (in FB376).

One week after this success No 65 Sqn, led by Flt Lt Foster, escorted Mosquitos of the Banff Wing against shipping in a fjord south of Alesund – some 500 miles from base! As they approached the coast and began the attack 14 Bf 109s of 10./JG 5, with a top cover of Fw 190s, approached from out of the sun and went for the Mosquitos. The Mustang IIIs turned on the attackers, and west of Alesund Flt Lt Graham Pearson (in HB823), having had one inconclusive combat, sighted more aircraft;

'I saw a formation of ME 109s at about 7000 ft and four of these peeled off to attack me. I took evasive action and the four broke – three to starboard and one to port. I went for the one that had broken to port and chased him in decreasing circles, firing at intervals but seeing only a few strikes on his tail. I then held my fire until within 40 yards of him, when I gave a five-second burst, smothering it in strikes. He burst

While engaged on escorts to coastal strike aircraft in the spring of 1945, No 19 Sqn began receiving 'bubble hooded' Mustang IVs such as KH655/QV-P. This aircraft was flown by Flt Lt Furneaux on the unit's first operations with a mixed force of Mk IIIs and IVs on 3 April (*No 19 Sqn Records*)

into flames and bailed out – I saw him going down in his parachute immediately above the target ship.'

Flt Lt Fred Bradford (in HB841) shot down another while Johnny Foster (again in FB376) shared a third Bf 109, as he described;

'I engaged one, bouncing him from line astern. The '109 was attacking the Mosquitos at the time, and I gave him several short squirts from line astern, immediately observing strikes near the tail. The '109 turned to port, and I gave him approximately a three- to four-second burst, again observing strikes all over the fuselage. The '109 straightened up and I closed in to approximately 50 yards, firing another two- to three-second burst, and his hood fell away, together with large pieces of fuselage. The '109's engine cut, and I overshot him, during which time my No 2 had a squirt. I then flew alongside the aircraft and watched the pilot bail out.'

He shared this victory with WO Abbott, and they noted, 'Interestingly, the top cover did not interfere!'

The following week No 19 Sqn also moved up to Peterhead, flying its first coastal strike escort for Beaufighters on a shipping sweep on 21 February. The mission was led by the CO, but it was aborted due to bad weather. They had better luck on 7 March, however, when in reasonable weather they escorted 44 Mosquitos on a successful shipping strike in the Kattegat. By now some bubble-hooded Mustang IVs were being delivered to the Peterhead squadrons, with No 65 Sqn flying its first example on operations on 8 March.

Four days later Sqn Ldr Hearne led No 19 Sqn on an escort for 44 Mosquitos that were sent to strike the Skagerrak. At 1645 hrs, as the force withdrew in the face of thick fog in the area some 25 miles southeast of Lister, they were bounced by ten Bf 109s from 13./JG 5, and the Mustang III flown by Sqn Ldr M R Hill went down. However, in the turning fight southeast of Lister Peter Hearne (KH511) shot one down, using just 160 rounds of ammunition. He wrote;

'I gave the order to drop tanks and turned to starboard across the Mosquitos, climbing to 3000 ft in the direction of the attack. I saw them intercept "Green" section almost immediately, spotting two ME 109s amongst them turning in tight circles. One ME 109 had both his wheels down. This did not seem to cramp his style, however, as he was turning as tightly as some of the Mustangs, and firing repeatedly. I got onto this aircraft's tail, following it round for some three tight orbits to starboard, firing two short bursts from about 150 yards and seeing strikes on its starboard wing root on the second occasion, until it straightened out temporarily. Just as he was going into another step turn to starboard I got in a good one-and-a-half-second burst from 300 yards. Black smoke came from his engine and the aircraft went immediately into a steep dive straight into the sea.'

James Butler (in KH450) also claimed one probably destroyed, although Luftwaffe records show that this too was lost. No 65 Sqn flew its first operation solely with Mustang IVs on the 17th, and used them again on 25 March in a combined escort with No 19 Sqn that was led by wing leader Wg Cdr Peter Wickham. The formation was attacked off the coast and No 65 Sqn claimed three destroyed and two damaged, although the unit lost its CO, Sqn Ldr Ian Stewart. Peter Wickham was also credited with one damaged, which was the last claim of his distinguished career;

'Just as we were leaving the coast I saw 17 Fw 190s (short-nosed) at 3000 ft ahead and coming towards us. I warned the Mosquitos, dropped my tanks and dived to attack. The FWs broke left and right, about five coming round onto my tail and the rest turning after the Mosquitos. Two of the FWs broke right as I began to catch up. I went after the No 1, whilst my No 4 shot down the No 2. I scored hits on the nose and right wing of the FW, who was jinking. The enemy aircraft fluttered down in a right hand turn towards the sea, and both my No 2 and myself thought he was finished – however, he recovered, and a long dogfight ensued. After ten or twelve minutes I broke off the engagement.'

His closing comment was a real compliment to his unknown adversary;

'This was, I think, the leader, and he was extremely good and aggressive. These were, on the whole, the best drilled and most aggressive pilots I have yet met.'

Flt Lt Foster was promoted to lead No 65 Sqn, and on 29 March it covered Mosquitos attacking shipping at Utvaer. The unit was engaged by 20+ Fw 190s, two of which were destroyed – these escort missions then continued throughout April. On the 5th, in excellent visibility, both squadrons rendezvoused with the Dallachy Wing's Beaufighters and headed for the Norwegian coast. Later, as they were crossing the coast off

Laden with long-range tanks, Mustang IVs of No 65 Sqn prepare for take-off from RAF Peterhead on one of the unit's final wartime missions (*Roger Freeman*)

Vaasgo, homeward-bound, 15+ Bf 109s approached and were promptly engaged. Four of them were shot down, with one falling to Flt Lt Graham Pearson in Mustang IV KH465, who spotted a Beaufighter under attack;

'On my approach the '109 broke to port and I got in a four-second burst from 450 yards down to 50 yards, with a number of strikes. I then pulled over the aircraft, which was badly hit and pouring glycol. I was myself bounced and had to break to port – it was another Mustang. I then turned back towards Norway, and about seven miles from the coast I spotted a single '109 returning on the deck. Opening up, I overtook him about one mile off the coast and went round two turns, firing bursts from 200 yards down to 50 yards. I saw strikes on the engine, which gave off slight smoke. He jettisoned his hood and attempted to ditch, and on striking the water his aircraft entirely disintegrated.'

Flg Off Black (in KH715) also claimed a Bf 109 shot down, while the new CO, Sqn Ldr Johnny Foster (in KH788), made his final claim when he intercepted a Messerschmitt that was attacking a Beaufighter;

'I dived down and met one head on coming in to attack. I gave him a very short burst, and when he passed me I broke to starboard and got on his tail, closing from 400 yards into 150 yards, firing a 7-8 second burst. I immediately observed strikes all round the cockpit and wing roots, and he developed a rather severe glycol leak. I overshot and my No 2 saw him strike the water and disintegrate.'

Finally, Flt Lt 'Maxie' Lloyd (in KH685) was credited with a probable – his fifth and final claim in an RAF Mustang. Sadly, over the Danish coast on the way home Flt Lt James Butler of No 19 Sqn was hit by ground fire and crashed into the sea in flames.

The wing claimed another victory two days later when No 19 Sqn provided a dozen Mustang IIIs as close escort to a force of two-dozen Beaufighters, while four more Mustang IVs from No 65 Sqn pushed ahead of them in a sweep. Soon after the strike aircraft had attacked two vessels in Vadheim Fjord about ten Fw 190s appeared from the south and the Mustang III/IVs promptly dropped their underwing tanks and engaged. No 65 Sqn pilot Graham Pearson (in KH686) recalled;

'I dived about 1000 ft to gain speed and then passed under the formation, pulling up and attacking the rear man of their port section. I noticed a number of strikes on his fuselage and the '190 in question flicked onto its back and dove straight down to the deck. I followed him straight into a small valley and did steep turns between 0-100 ft round several small log huts. I had a big advantage over him, and got in several bursts from 200 yards down to 50 yards, seeing a number of strikes. After five minutes another '190 came down and delivered a head-on attack, but did not hit me. The original '190 was blazing underneath by this time, and in a final half-turn with him I scored more hits at close range. He crashed into the ground and burst into flames.'

Pearson then went after the other Fw 190 that was flying low up a valley, and when his fire struck home it flicked over and crashed into the hillside. These victories took Pearson's tally of claims to four kills and one probable, but frustratingly his fifth confirmed victory never came. Nevertheless, with three Mustang IV kills, he was the RAF's most successful pilot in this version of the US fighter. Flg Off Bill Black also made his fifth claim when he damaged another of the Fw 190s. However,

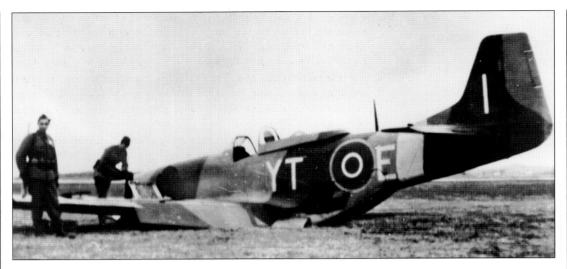

during a sortie soon afterwards, Graham Pearson's aircraft suffered an engine failure and he force-landed in Sweden on 19 April. Interned for a short time, he was awarded a DFC upon his return to the UK.

Eight days earlier, on 11 April, it was No 19 Sqn's turn to escort a Beaufighter wing that had been sent to attack shipping off the southern tip of Norway. As the Mustang IVs were flying low over the coast Sqn Ldr Hearne (in KH511) sighted four Bf 109s over Lister airfield. Chasing after one of them, he shot down the *Staffelführer* of 16./JG 5, Ltn Adolf Gillet, some three miles from the airfield to claim his fourth victory. Hearne commented afterwards;

'The '109s we encountered were obviously an experienced bunch of boys. Their turning circle is decidedly better than ours at low speed. The lowering of 20 degrees of flap may just enable us to hold them in the turn, although I feel they could outclimb us.'

Three days later, shortly before 1330 hrs, No 19 Sqn, led by Sqn Ldr Hearne (in KH511), provided an escort for 18 Beaufighters of the Dallachy Wing to Josing Fjord, despite poor weather at Peterhead. His memorable combat was recounted in his report;

'After covering the last of the Beaufighters out over the coast from Josing Fjord, I led the squadron eastward to sweep around Lister at 5000 ft until I came to Fede Fjord. I observed one aircraft airborne over Lister flying very low in a westerly direction. He was, in fact, beating up the aerodrome, because he pulled up to 400 ft over his base, turned very steeply right (emitting a trail of black smoke) and headed due north for the hill just north of Lister. I intercepted him about one-and-half miles off shore northwest of his base.

'I identified the aircraft as an Me 109, and attacked it from the port quarter with a large angle off but saw no results. The Me 109, once aware of the situation, pulled his wheels up and gave an amazing display of combat flying, which had he been luckier might have ended disastrously for one or even two of our aircraft. Although heavily outnumbered, and with a reasonably good chance of bridging the 1.5 miles of sea and seeking the protection of his heavily defended base, he chose to fight it out to the last, firing on every single occasion he could bring his guns to bear.

Mustang IV KH695/YT-E force-landed at Getteron, on the west coast of Sweden, on 19 April 1945 after it suffered engine failure during an escort mission over the Skagerrak. It was being flown at the time by Flt Lt Graham Pearson, who had four victories and a probable – all on Mustangs – to his credit. He is believed to be the top-scoring RAF Mustang IV pilot (*No 65 Sqn Records*)

I damaged him slightly in my second burst as a thin trail of white smoke began to issue from his port wing root. I then broke off and circled above him while other Mustangs that were eager to kill, pounced on the Me 109. None of them could get sufficient deflection on him, and I chose an appropriate opportunity to come down on him in a tight turn to port and at an angle of about 70 degrees. Firing a short burst from 200 yards, I saw a red glow appear in his cockpit and he gently rolled over and went vertically into the sea.'

Having claimed his fifth victory against what he considered to be a particularly skilful pilot – almost certainly Gefrieter Bahlmann of 13./JG 5 – Peter Hearne thus became the last pilot to 'make ace' on the Mustang III/IV. This was also the last engagement fought with the Lister fighters. During their periods on escort work in the last months of the war No 19 Sqn had claimed three confirmed kills (all by the CO) and a probable, while No 65 Sqn, which had seen more action, was credited with 14 destroyed and eight probables against a loss of three in combat.

INDUSTRIAL TARGETS

The first three Mustang IVs for No 154 Sqn arrived at RAF Biggin Hill, in Kent, during the morning of 3 February 1945, although the unit's CO led an escort with their Spitfire VIIs in the afternoon. Bad weather then reduced the level of operations for the rest of the month, so squadron pilots did a lot of local flying in order to familiarise themselves with their new mounts.

3 February also saw Nos 234 and 309 Sqns perform a sweep of the Hanover-Brunswick area, while No 316 Sqn took part in a 'Rodeo' further south over the Frankfurt area, where several ground targets were

Maj Werner Christie stands in front of his personal aircraft, FB344/AZ-Z, when CO of No 234 Sqn. He was flying it on 9 February 1945 when he shot down an Ar 96 over Treuchtlingen to claim his first victory with the Mustang III (*via Steve Brooking*)

strafed. There then followed a series of escorts and sweeps to various parts of western Germany, but on the 9th Werner Christie (in FB344) took No 234 Sqn as far as Munich in the hope that they would catch enemy aircraft unawares, thinking themselves safe so far to the south. Eight aircraft set out, and having strafed some Ju 290s seen on the ground, they then spotted three Ar 96 trainers that were practising air combat over Treuchtlingen – '234 were happy to help them with this', one pilot later noted! Dropping his long-range tanks, Flt Sgt Stan Farmiloe went after an Arado, but in his excitement overshot the first two before lining up on the third;

'It went into a deep spiral dive towards the deck. The German then made the grievous error of pulling up, allowing me to open fire with a perfect, and decisive, two-second burst from 200 yards. Both pilots quickly bailed out of the clearly stricken aeroplane before it plunged into a wood.'

Flt Sgt Fred Stewart claimed the second Ar 96 and the last fell to Christie, who claimed his first, and only, success with the Mustang III;

'I was at 2000 ft, so I pulled up to engage and dropped my tanks. I noticed one Ar 96 peel off and dive down to about 100 ft. I followed with my No 2. The aircraft had seen us because it was weaving violently. I fired a few bursts with extreme deflection. I closed to 200 yards and fired with a two- to three-second burst and deflection of 45 to 30 degrees to port. I observed strikes on the aircraft's port wing and then on the cockpit and engine. It burst into flames and crashed in an open field.'

These were in the event No 234

Sqn's final victories of the war, frustratingly taking the unit's overall total to 99 aircraft destroyed! It was also Werner Christie's swansong, as the following day he took over as wing leader at Andrews Field. He was only the second Norwegian to be promoted to such a position in the RAF. Christie's successor at No 234 Sqn was 13-kill ace Sqn Ldr 'Jas' Storrar.

A few days later, on 14 February, No 118 Sqn flew its first Mustang III operation when Sqn Ldr 'Nip' Heppell led a dozen aircraft as part of the escort to an abortive Lancaster attack on a viaduct near Paderborn. That same day No 126 Sqn received a new CO when Norwegian ace Maj Arne Austeen took over, while at Andrews Field Grp Capt Nowierski handed over control of the wing to another successful Polish pilot, Grp Capt Tadeusz Rolski.

In early 1945 Flt Lt Stanislaw Blok was a flight commander with No 315 Sqn, and on 21 February he shot down an Fw 190 during an escort over Germany to become an ace (*Elgin Scott via W Ratuszynski*)

Blok achieved his distinction when flying Mustang III KH492/PK-U, which is seen here taxiing out at RAF Andrews Field at the start of yet another mission a few weeks later (*via Wojtek Matusiak*)

Both wings contributed to the escort to a heavy raid on Wesel on the
19th that was also Austeen's first operation with No 126 Sqn. Two days
later Hanover was the target, and during the associated sweep the Poles
found some success. Led by Sqn Ldr Jozef Zulikowski, the wing took off
in mid afternoon with No 306 Sqn in front, followed by No 315 then
No 309. Looking for targets of opportunity east of Salzwedel, Zulikowski
spotted a solitary Fw 190 that he promptly shot down, while Flt Lt
Troczynski of No 306 Sqn destroyed an unfortunate Do 217 that he
intercepted in the same area.

Penetrating as far as Osnabrück, the Poles then clashed with 40+ long-
nosed Fw 190Ds that split into two groups. A series of individual
dogfights then ensued, and during this action Flt Lt Stanislaw Blok
(in KH492) and his section from No 315 Sqn remained high as top cover.
However, upon spotting a solitary Fw 190 on the tail of a Mustang III
he dived at the German fighter, firing a short burst from 400 yards and
seeing many hits on the fuselage. Blok did not follow as it dived away,
but soon afterwards spotted a *Rotte* of Fw 190s and closed into their
'six o'clock'. He fired a long burst at one, which exploded, thus giving him
his fifth victory. This also made Blok the last Polish pilot to become an ace
on the Mustang III.

Squadronmate Flg Off Haczkiewicz chased one onto the deck and
brought it down just east of Osnabrück, while No 315 Sqn's Flt Sgt
Cempel destroyed another with a short burst from 200 yards, causing
it to disintegrate. Several Mustang IIIs were lost, however. No 309 Sqn
was also successful, Flt Sgt 'Toni' Murkowski at last claiming the unit's
first Mustang III victory when he shot down an Fw 190D some 25 miles
east of Etricht.

Close escort, 'Ramrods' or 'Rodeos' continued to occupy both wings,
with the Bielefeld Viaduct, Dortmund-Ems Canal, oil targets on the
Ruhr and marshalling yards at Mainz all being targets through the rest
of the month, but with little action coming their way. By this stage,
however, fuel shortages and a lack of radar cover meant that much of the
still potent Luftwaffe defences were concentrated further to the east.
At month-end intelligence indicated that there might be further flying
bomb attacks on London launched from Holland and, perhaps because
of their experience the previous summer, the Poles were directed from

first light on 28 February to maintain one squadron at 'Readiness' and two squadrons 'Available'. The standby continued for a couple of weeks.

At the beginning of March a new wing began to form when Mustang IV-equipped No 154 Sqn moved to RAF Hunsdon, in Hertfordshire, where it joined No 611 'West Lancashire' Sqn. This unit had also just begun converting to Mustang IVs, and it became operational on the 23rd. On 8 March Lt Col Werner Christie arrived to lead the wing, Flt Lt Bill Fleming recalling his arrival to the author;

'The wing leader at Hunsdon was a Norwegian, Lt Col W "Cloudy" Christie. His nickname came from the fact that he had us flying on every conceivable occasion, whether we were on ops or not, and even if the cloud was down to the deck. The story went around that Norwegian pilots, in addition to their normal pay, received a bonus for every hour flown!'

The first Mustang IV operation for No 154 Sqn was on 9 March, and it was to be led by the CO, Sqn Ldr Gerry Stonhill. The unit had been briefed to escort Lancasters to Remlinghausen, and when Stonhill was forced to return early, Flt Lt Ted Andrews assumed the lead. Further operations followed almost daily, with Christie in his personally marked Mustang IV WHC often leading. One of the unit's few combat losses occurred on 12 March when Flt Lt Ted Andrews went down, as he recalled to the author;

'I had an engine failure whilst at more than 35,000 ft near Dortmund, which was being bombed that day. We had not seen the ground since leaving London because of total cloud cover. I got bearings on the VHF and glided west until the ground station said I must bail out, as I was probably by then west of the Rhine and back over Allied-occupied territory. I followed their instructions, but when I landed I discovered that I was still in German territory and was captured. Whilst a prisoner I was wounded by rocket-firing Typhoons, which was not an experience to be enjoyed.'

Operations against the by now rapidly shrinking Reich continued in improving weather, with the Allied armies closing on the Rhine – the last great natural barrier in the west.

In mid-March Danish ace Wg Cdr Kaj Birksted was appointed as wing commander flying of the Bentwaters Wing, which continued to escort the 'heavies' against a wide range of targets throughout the western part of Germany, but on the 21st came a different mission. Bomber Command's No 2 Group had planned a daring pinpoint raid (codenamed Operation *Carthage*) on Shell House, in the centre of Copenhagen, which was home to the HQ of the feared *Gestapo* secret police. It was thought that the latter were about to conduct a series of mass arrests of the Danish resistance. The operation was flown by three Mosquito squadrons that were escorted by Mustangs IIIs from Nos 64 and 126 Sqns – these units also acted in the anti-flak role. The raid was a spectacular success, although several Mosquitos and two Mustang IIIs were lost, one being flown by Flt Lt David Drew of No 64 Sqn. His fighter received a direct hit from anti-aircraft fire and crashed into the city in flames.

Escorts continued through the month – often to Ruhr targets – but usually with little action for the fighters, although flak and the possibility of engine failure were constant hazards. The first major attack by enemy

For the last two months of the war in Europe the Bentwaters Wing was led by US-born Danish ace Lt Col Kaj Birksted, who also led the last coastal strike escorts. He made an emotional return to his native land in his personal Mustang IV a few days after hostilities had ceased (*via C F Shores*)

jets on an RAF bomber formation came during a mission by 100+ Lancasters to Bremen on 23 March. The Mustang IIIs countered, however, making several claims. Shortly after 1000 hrs just off the target in a clear sky with a slight haze, the bombers came under attack by some 15-20 Me 262s that were in turn engaged by a section from No 118 Sqn. Three jets were damaged, one by Flt Lt Mike Giddings (in KN503);

'I led my section down on a ME 262. I fired very short bursts at this and two other ME 262s in the same area at extreme range, observing no strikes. As we turned to rejoin the bombers I dived on another ME 262 that was turning below me, and I fired a 2-3 second burst from 700 yards down to 500 yards, seeing a couple of strikes and part of the starboard wing root fly off. It was impossible to close the range of these attackers.'

Giddings, who later became an air marshal, fired 60 rounds from his four guns. Sgt Aleksander Pietrzak (in SR418) from No 309 Sqn also damaged one, while Flg Off Albert Yeardley, who had only joined No 126 Sqn on 6 March, got close enough to put a well-aimed burst into one. The jet went straight in, Yeardley's third victory also being the first Me 262 to be shot down by an RAF Mustang III/IV.

The following day all the wings were out in force to cover the airborne element of Operation *Varsity* – the airborne crossing of the Rhine near Wesel. Although some gliders were shot down by ground fire, there was little to report during a five-hour mission. On 25 March Flt Lt Bibrowicz shot down No 315 Sqn's last V1, with the last flying bomb to reach England being recorded on the 29th. Two days earlier Lt Col Christie had led the Hunsdon Wing on an escort to Hamm, and after completing this part of the mission the wing returned to sweep the Lübeck area. By then cloud had drifted in, and beneath the widespread overcast visibility was poor. Nevertheless, the wing encountered a number of Fw 190s, and Flt Lt Phil Knowles of No 154 Sqn recalled the ensuing melee to the author;

'On 27 March we escorted Lancasters bombing Hamm. Climbing out through thick bumpy cloud layers was rather unpleasant. It was vital not to lose sight of your lead aircraft, and this meant maintaining tight formation. It was said that our wing commander particularly disliked this kind of weather, and was therefore known as "Cloudy" Christie.

'After the bombers had left for home we went on a sweep in the Brunswick-Lübeck area, where we bounced a close formation of 15 Fw 190s, well below us. Col Christie was leading the squadron, and he destroyed two – which I saw hit the ground – and damaged one.

Having escorted 'Father of the RAF' Lord Trenchard to Germany on 2 June 1945, four Mustang IIIs of No 118 Sqn stayed the night at B156 Lüneburg. The second aircraft visible is KN503/NK-Z in which Flt Lt Mike Giddings had his brief encounter with enemy jet fighters on 23 March 1945 (*B Harper*)

WO Bunting claimed one probable and Flt Lt Lee and Plt Off Todd each got one damaged.

'On the way down the CO congratulated his flight for sticking together. What he did not know was that his No 4 had broken off and his place had been taken by an Fw 190, who was banging away at the No 3, WO Vickery – his fighter was not seriously damaged, but had a number of shots fired through his fuel tanks. The self-sealing tanks were very effective, but he lost some fuel nevertheless. In spite of this Vickery pressed on and got home with virtually no fuel. We thought he was mad not to land and refuel in Belgium, especially since it was a 5 hrs 25 min total trip. Apparently he was getting married that weekend and didn't want to miss the wedding! One shot had gone through the red of the fuselage roundel and then passed between the doubled up elevator control wires, pushing them apart.'

Other escorts were then flown to the end of the month, but the mission flown on 31 March was No 154 Sqn's last, as it was ordered to pass its aircraft on to No 442 Sqn and disband. Some Me 262s attacked the formation on this date, but their speed made them impossible to engage. Nevertheless, the CO did fire at one – more in hope than expectation! One of the pilots on the mission was Flg Off Bill Fleming, who recalled;

'My most memorable experience involving the Me 262 occurred during an escort mission with over 450 RAF "heavies" to Hamburg, attacking the Blohm und Voss U-boat building yards. South of the target I noticed some vapour trails several thousand feet above us going down in the same direction. I reported these to the CO, who said that they were probably Mosquito pathfinders, but to keep an eye on them.

'Shortly afterwards I observed several Me 262s diving through our formation from above and behind, travelling at high speed. We dropped our tanks and dived on them, but before getting within range they opened fire on the leading bombers with what looked like rocket projectiles and cannon, scoring hits on at least two of the "heavies". One of the Me 262 pilots came back under us after he finished his attack run, and "Red" section, led by the CO, turned on our backs and went straight down after him at high speed. We opened fire at extreme range before he pulled away with his superior speed.'

Also engaged was Albert Yeardley of No 126 Sqn, who managed to damage one of the jets.

No 154 Sqn received Mustang IVs in place of its Spitfire VIIs at RAF Biggin Hill in February 1945. Among the aircraft supplied was this one, seen on the wing on 18 February whilst being flown by Flg Off Palmer. KH765 was also regularly flown by Flt Lt Norman Lee, who was in it on 27 March 1945 when, in the Lübeck area, No 154 Sqn had a melee that resulted in Lt Col Werner Christie claiming two Fw 190s destroyed and Lee sharing another damaged with Plt Off Todd (*E Andrews*)

With No 154 Sqn's disbandment, its pilots were dispersed to other units, some going to No 126 Sqn. On 3 April the latter unit was in action over Mulhausen when, in the late afternoon, Flg Off Kingsbury destroyed a Bf 109G. His CO, Maj Arne Austeen witnessed his unit's last victory;

'I saw an ME 109G diving at me with my No 3 on his tail. I broke hard against him, and he did not seem to try to follow me around. A few seconds later I saw the '109 straighten up from his turn and my No 3 open fire, obtaining strikes in the port wing root, engine cowling and cockpit. The aircraft started burning and dived in flames vertically into clouds at about 3000 ft. I confirm one ME 109G destroyed.'

That same day the iconic Polish fighter unit No 303 Sqn arrived at Andrews Field under its ace CO, Sqn Ldr 'Gandy' Drobinski, and began re-equipping with Mustang IVs. There were also several other changes to command during the month, with No 129 Sqn being taken over by Sqn Ldr Mike Giddings from No 118 Sqn, while on the 6th Sqn Ldr Wladislaw Potocki assumed leadership of No 315 Sqn.

No 442 Sqn's first Mustang IV operation was on 9 April when it supported a raid on the Rasburg oil refinery. The mission was led by Lt Col Christie. The other wings covered a raid on the U-boat works at Hamburg, where just short of the target the Lancasters were attacked by 20+ Me 262s. On their first pass the jets sent three of the bombers down. With No 315 Sqn remaining high, Nos 306 and 309 Sqns went after the jets. No 306 Sqn's CO, Sqn Ldr Jozef Zulikowski, was able to claim his third, and final, victory, and the last of 68 for his squadron. The honours, however, went to No 309 Sqn, which during the subsequent fight had the distinction of claiming the final Polish kills of the war. They were indeed significant scalps, for Flt Lt Gorzula, Flt Lt Mencel and WO Murkowski (in FB385) each destroyed one of the jets. Murkowski damaged another, while a fifth was damaged by Flg Offs Mozlowski and Lewandowski. 'Toni' Murkowski told the author about this encounter;

'During this raid on Hamburg we were off on the right, and suddenly the jets appeared from behind. I was in a turn and managed to slip behind one. Gaining in speed, I opened up when I got to within 200 yards of the Me 262. I could see bits flying off the engine, and perhaps the flaps too, and he just dived in from about 20,000 ft. I then caught another, though I thought that I had seen two. The Me 262s were much better than our Mustangs, and if they had just flown straight and level I'd never have caught them. It was quite a short mission – only 3 hrs 30 min – the worse part of which was several hours sat on a hard parachute. Funnily enough, I recently met an air gunner from one of the Lancasters who showed me a photo of a Mustang diving through the bombers, and when we compared logbooks it was of me chasing the first '262!'

Jets were encountered by No 234 Sqn's Mustang IIIs on 10 April too when 200 'heavies' were escorted to Leipzig – the deepest penetration into Germany to date. No 118 Sqn met some Me 163 Komet rocket fighters as well, but they proved far too fast to allow an interception. Four Mustang IVs from No 611 Sqn optimistically chased one nevertheless!

However, the wing did gain the RAF's only success against the Me 163 later that same day when one was shot down by Flg Off John 'Slops' Haslop of No 165 Sqn. Having spotted the rocket fighter, he 'firewalled' the throttle of his Mustang III and dived after it, opening fire as he did so.

On 21 February 1945 Flt Sgt 'Toni' Murkowski claimed No 309 Sqn's first air combat victory in the Mustang III when he shot down an Fw 190D 25 miles east of Etricht. A few weeks later on 9 April he was part of an escort to Hamburg when No 309 Sqn engaged a group of Me 262s and he claimed one of the four jets shot down – the final Polish victories of the war. Murkowski also damaged a second jet fighter too (*A Murkowski*)

He then valiantly attempted to follow the diminutive enemy fighter when it zoom climbed, but he blacked out due to the excessive 'g'. Haslop duly set a course for home, his Mustang III having several more degrees of wing dihedral and wrinkled skinning after his escapade. Upon his return to base Haslop was told that several bomber crews had seen the Me 163 dive into the ground following his attempted interception, so he was credited with the RAF's only combat victory over this unique aircraft, and awarded the DFC.

Bomber Command's daylight raids were now penetrating ever deeper into Germany, and on 11 April Wg Cdr Birksted, in Mustang III 'KB', led an escort to Nuremburg – he would fly regularly with No 118 Sqn on escorts throughout the month. Bomber Command also made several raids against the remnants of the Kriegsmarine's surface fleet, with the hulk of the *Gneisenau* being bombed in Stettin and, on the 16th, the *Lutzow* being targeted in Swinemünde. Flg Off Phil Knowles was on the latter mission, and he told the author;

'We provided escort cover to Swinemünde, where bombers were targeting the pocket battleship *Lutzow*, formerly the *Deutschland*. We went with 20 Lancasters, and we were a little late in making the rendezvous with them over Europe. They called up to say that if we did not meet up in five minutes they were going home! We met okay, the weather was clear over the target and they bombed successfully. The flak over the target was extremely intense and a number of "Lancs" were lost. It was a terrible sight to see such a big machine spiralling down in flames with bits falling off. We heard later that the *Lutzow* had been sunk. Swinemünde was fairly close to the Russians, and we could hear them clearly on the R/T.'

The only Me 163 Komet rocket fighter to be shot down by the RAF in air combat fell to the guns of a Mustang III of No 165 Sqn on 10 April 1945. Aircraft from the unit are seen here taxiing out at RAF Bentwaters at the start of another late-war mission. Photographs of aircraft from this unit are particularly elusive (*via C H Goss*)

No 442 Sqn only had one combat while flying Mustang IVs, and this took place on 16 April 1945. The unit emerged from the clash with a solitary victory, Flg Offs L H Wilson (who was flying KH647/Y2-H seen here) and Robillard sharing in the destruction of an Fw 190 (*A J Malladaine*)

No 611 Sqn's only action with the Mustang IV came on the same day as No 442 Sqn's, although it was more successful, claiming six destroyed, one probable and two damaged. During that mission KH746/FY-R was flown by Flg Off Wilding, who did not register a claim, however (*B Partridge*)

Other aircraft from No 118 Sqn then conducted a sweep with No 442 Sqn, which had its first, and only, action in the Mustang IV. In hazy weather to the northeast of Berlin at 1745 hrs the unit bounced some Fw 190s, and during the 15-minute fight that followed one of the German fighters was destroyed by Flg Offs Wilson and Robillard, while a second was probably destroyed by Flt Lt Shenk. Wilson reported;

'"Yellow 2" (Flg Off Robillard) and I chased a Fw 190. "Yellow 2" gave a short burst, strikes seen, but he got out of position to continue the combat. I was about 1000 yards away, closing rapidly to 250 yards, and I gave the fighter a two-second burst with five-tenths degree deflection. The enemy aircraft caught fire and crashed into a small wood, exploding.'

No 316 Sqn was giving withdrawal cover for the Swinemünde mission, and it gave chase to an Me 410 but lost sight of it at sea level.

The most significant action of 16 April, however, was found by No 611 Sqn, which was being being led by Werner Christie. After seeing the bombers safely away, Christie led the squadron on a sweep over Berlin, initially encountering some Soviet *Shturmoviks* and their Yak escort. Later, in a clear sky with a heat haze at about 10,000 ft in the vicinity of Finow airfield, about 20 Fw 190s were spotted. Christie, flying his personal Mustang IV KH790, attacked one and shot off half of its wing, after which the fighter rolled over and crashed. It was the Norwegian ace's final victory, and also the last to be claimed by an RAF ace in a Mustang. Christie wrote afterwards;

'I opened up, firing a five-second burst at the leading aircraft in a formation of three, range 150 yards, deflection five-tenths of a degree to starboard, and observed strikes on the port side of the engine and cockpit. I also saw that his starboard wingtip had been damaged. The aircraft was then smoking badly and gliding straight ahead. I pulled out to the port side and made a second attack, opening up at 200 yards and closing in to about 50 yards, ending up dead astern. I fired several short bursts lasting ten seconds, and during the attack I saw strikes on the cockpit, engine and both wings. The port wing fell off and port wheel fell down. It then did five or six quick rolls horizontally and crashed in flames in a wood.'

Christie then reformed his section, noting many aircraft, including Me 262s parked, on an airfield below. In the same action that the Norwegian claimed his kill Flt Lt Partridge of No 611 Sqn also destroyed an Fw 190, as did WO Ken Mack, although the honours went to Flg Off George Jones (in KM150), who got two. He recalled;

'I was dead astern of an enemy aircraft at about 280 mph and opened fire, giving it a five-second burst. Pieces flew past me and oil covered my windscreen. I then saw more strikes on the fuselage and the Fw 190 burst into flames, dived and blew up on hitting the ground in a nearby wood.

'I then saw another one well below me, heading towards an airfield. I gave chase for three minutes until I was 200 yards astern. I gave it a short burst but scored no hits, so I fired another short burst. I saw strikes on the fuselage and mainplane, so continued to fire until it began to disintegrate. I followed it down and saw it crash to the ground.'

In the squadron's last combat with the Luftwaffe it had claimed five destroyed with two probables and one damaged. They were also the last confirmed victories by RAF Mustangs.

By now No 234 Sqn was equipped with Mustang IVs, with 'Jas' Storrar flying one on the 18 April mission that also involved the Hunsdon Wing, as recalled by Flg Off Knowles of No 126 Sqn;

'On 18 April we escorted 950 Lancasters and Halifaxes attacking Heligoland. The weather was clear and the bombing accurate and intense on such a small target. It was difficult to believe that any of the island could remain. We heard that Col Christie, our "Wingco" at Biggin Hill and Hunsdon, was hit by flak and bailed out over Schleswig-Holstein.'

In fact Christie's aircraft had suffered an engine fire and he was forced to bail out over enemy territory near Handorf to became a PoW for a short time – he was replaced by 'Jas' Storrar. The following day came a mission to Munich, during which Flt Lt Janusz Walawski (in KH493) of No 316 Sqn destroyed an Me 410 and an He 111 on the ground at Memmingen. Then on the 25th Bomber Command made its final raid on the Berchtesgaden, which involved all of the squadrons, including No 303, led by Drobinski, flying one of its very few Mustang IV operations. To everyone's chagrin, however, no enemy fighters were seen. The Luftwaffe had been virtually destroyed.

Laden with underwing tanks, Mustang III FB181/SZ-R of No 316 Sqn taxies out for another escort mission from Andrews Field in the spring of 1945 (*Elgin Scott via W Ratuszynski*)

1
Mustang I AG470/RU-M of Flg Off H Hills, No 414 Sqn RCAF, Croydon, 19 August 1942

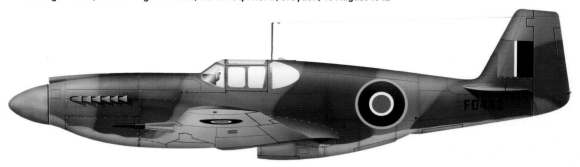

2
Mustang IA FD442 of Sqn Ldr J A F Maclachlan, AFDU, Duxford, 29 June 1945

3
Mustang III FB113/QV-H of Flt Lt D P Lamb, No 19 Sqn, Gravesend, 15 February 1944

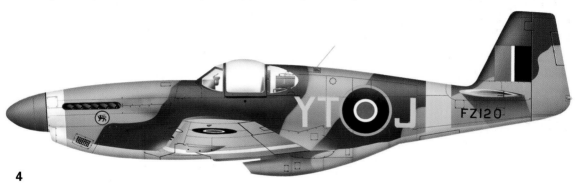

4
Mustang III FZ120/YT-J of Sqn Ldr D H Westenra, No 65 Sqn, Ford and Funtington, April-May 1944

5
Mustang III FB125/DV-F of Flt Lt D F Ruchwaldy, No 129 Sqn, Coolham, April-May 1944

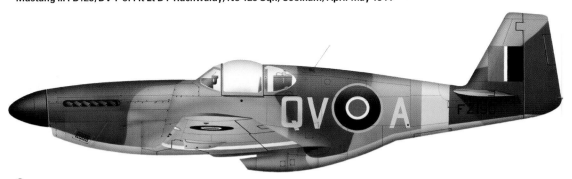

6
Mustang III FZ190/QV-A of WO M H Bell, No 19 Sqn, Funtington, 9 May 1944

7
Mustang III FB201/QV-D of Sqn Ldr W M Gilmore, No 19 Sqn, Funtington, 29 May 1944

8
Mustang III FB169/DV-H of Sqn Ldr C Haw, No 129 Sqn, Coolham, 6 June 1944

9
Mustang III FZ196/UZ-D of Flt Lt W Potoki, No 306 Sqn, Coolham, 7 June 1944

10
Mustang III FB145/PK-F of Flt Sgt J Bargielowski, No 315 Sqn, Coolham, 12 June 1944

11
Mustang III FB226/MT-K of Flg Off C L F Talalla, No 122 Sqn, Ford, 12 June 1944

12
Mustang III FZ114/MT-A of Flg Off M H Pinches, No 122 Sqn, Ford, 17 June 1944

13
Mustang III FB260/LW of Lt Col L A Wilmot, No 239 Wg, Falerium and Iesi, Italy, June-August 1944

14
Mustang III FB337/AK-A of Sqn Ldr S R Whiting, No 213 Sqn, Leverano, Italy, July 1944

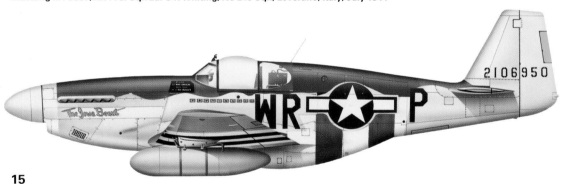

15
P-51B Mustang 42-106950/WR-P of Flt Lt W B Peglar, 354th FS/355th FG, Steeple Morden, July-August 1944

16
Mustang III HB886/TN of Grp Capt T Nowierski, No 133 (Polish) Wing, Brenzett, August 1944

17
Mustang III HB936/GA-A of Sgt A Banks, No 112 Sqn, Iesi, Italy, 29 August 1944

18
Mustang III HB952/GN-F of Sqn Ldr J te Kloot, No 249 Sqn, Canne, Italy, 28 September 1944

19
Thunderbolt I HB975/WK-L of Sqn Ldr L C C Hawkins, No 135 Sqn, Chittagong, India, October 1944-December 1944

20
Mustang III FB344/AZ-Z of Maj W H Christie, No 234 Sqn, Bentwaters, January-February 1945

21
Mustang IV KH681/GL-Z of Capt H J E Clarke, No 5 Sqn SAAF, Fano, Italy, December 1944-January 1945

22
Thunderbolt II HD292/ZT-L of Sqn Ldr N Cameron, No 258 Sqn, Ratnap, India, 11 February 1945

23
Mustang III KH570/5J-X of Maj A Austeen, No 126 Sqn, Bentwaters, 23 February 1945

24
Mustang III KH503/NK-Z of Flt Lt K C M Giddings, No 118 Sqn, Bentwaters, 23 March 1945

25
Mustang III KH574/WC-A of Sqn Ldr A Glowacki, No 309 Sqn, Andrews Field, April 1945

26
Mustang IV KH860/AZ-G of Sqn Ldr J A Storrar, No 234 Sqn, Bentwaters, April 1945

27
Mustang IV KH765/HG-R of Flt Lt N W Lee, No 154 Sqn, Hunsdon, March 1945

28
Thunderbolt II KJ348 of Grp Capt F R Carey, No 73 OTU, Fayid, Egypt, spring 1945

29
Mustang IV KM193/QV-J of Sqn Ldr P J Hearne, No 19 Sqn, Peterhead, April-May 1945

30
Mustang IV KH695/YT-E of Flt Lt G S Pearson, No 65 Sqn, 19 April 1945

31
Mustang IV KH826/AK-G of Flt Lt G S Hulse, No 213 Sqn, Biferno, Italy, 23 April 1945

32
Mustang IV KM121/MLD of Wg Cdr M L Donnet, Bentwaters Wing, Bentwaters, April 1945

33
Mustang IV KH729/Y2-A of Wg Cdr J A Storrar, No 442 Sqn, Hunsdon, 25 Apr 1945

34
Mustang IV KH676/CV-A of Flg Off A F Lane, No 3 Sqn RAAF, Cervia, Italy, April 1945

35
Mustang III HB876/9G-L of Flt Lt D H Kimball, No 441 Sqn RCAF, Digby, May 1945

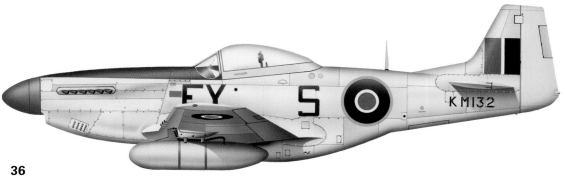

36
Mustang IV KM132/FY-S of Sqn Ldr P C P Farnes No 611 'West Lancashire' Sqn, Peterhead, 27 July 1945

ITALY AND THE BALKANS

The first Mustangs to serve with the RAF overseas were a pair of F-6As (equivalent to the Mk I) borrowed from the USAAF in the spring of 1943 by No 225 Sqn at Souk el Khemis, in Algeria, for photo-reconnaissance duties. They flew their first sorties over Tunis on 21 April, where they were intercepted by two Fw 190s but escaped unscathed. The range and performance of the Mustangs, however, soon led to more aggressive use.

Axis forces in North Africa surrendered on 13 May, and at this time the Marauder I crews of No 14 Sqn, based at Blida, also in Algeria, were regularly seeing formations of enemy transport aircraft on their missions over the Mediterranean. A number of these were shot down through the summer, with at least two falling to the unit CO, Wg Cdr Dick Maydwell. He in turn argued that a fighter flight within his squadron would give them the means to take more effective action. Consequently, No 14 Sqn was issued with four F-6As again drawn from USAAF stocks, as well as four fighter pilots to fly them, including Canadian Flg Off Harvey Crawford from No 32 Sqn.

The flight began operations on 29 May, and the very next day Crawford and Flt Sgt Campbell shot down a Ju 52/3m to claim the RAF Mustang's first victim in the Mediterranean. The unit diarist recorded;

'Mustangs 364 (Flg Off Crawford) and 414 (Flt Sgt Campbell) sighted two floatplanes, two Ju 52s and a Ju 53 (sic) off Cap Bellavista at 0725 hrs.

No 213 Sqn re-equipped with Mustang IIIs in the late spring of 1944 and flew a few missions with the aircraft from North Africa, including one on 14 June when Flt Lt Scott Vos took FB333/AK-N on a shipping reconnaissance to Rhodes harbour. The next day he flew it on an escort mission for SAAF Baltimores that also targeted Rhodes (*No 213 Sqn Records*)

364 attacked and engine fell out of Ju 52. 414 then attacked and Ju 52 went down towards the sea. When last seen it was just above the surface about 100 yards from the cliffs. Claim one Ju 52 destroyed.'

The Mustang had been 'blooded' in the Mediterranean, and Crawford went on to gain further success flying Spitfire IXs with No 411 Sqn in the latter half of 1944. Another victory was claimed on the 31 May when, off the eastern coast of Sardinia, Flt Lt Blair and Flg Off Gildner shot down an Italian Fiat RS.14 floatplane. A few days later No 14 Sqn moved to Protville, in Tunisia, from where on the 7th Blair and Gildner again found more action during an armed reconnaissance over the Gulf of Oristana, shooting down another RS.14. However, operations with the Mustangs then tailed off, and no more were flown after the middle of the month. The aircraft were subsequently passed on to the USAAF's 111th Observation Squadron.

Its excellent performance and range meant that the Merlin-engined Mustang III was seen as a suitable replacement for the Kittyhawks then serving in substantial numbers with RAF and Commonwealth units in the Mediterranean. The RAF in North Africa had thus not seen the last of the Mustang, for on 17 May 1944 No 213 Sqn, based at Idku in Egypt, received its first two Mustang IIIs to begin re-equipping, and by the end of the month it was partially operational. The squadron's first Mustang III operation was flown the next day, when a reconnaissance sweep was made of Candia harbour on Crete.

On 1 June four of No 213 Sqn's Mustang IIIs formed part of the escort for a subsequent strike on Candia harbour, the operation lasting several days until three vessels spotted here were sunk. The Mustang IIIs, led by unit CO Sqn Ldr Spencer Whiting, flew top cover, and when the close escort was drawn off they dived down to escort the Beaufighters, but were mistaken for Bf 109s! One result of this was that white identification bands were painted around the Mustang III's wings and tail.

The squadron had its first encounter with the Luftwaffe in its new Mustang IIIs that same day when, just after lunch, flight commander Flt Lt C S Vos scrambled after a Ju 88, but only the unit's Spitfire IX element engaged. The other flight commander in No 213 Sqn at this time was Flt Lt C D A 'Tigger' Smith, who had five claims, but as yet no confirmed victories.

On the 15th the CO led another escort for South African Air Force (SAAF) Baltimores that were attacking Rhodes, and No 213 Sqn spotted five Ar 196 floatplanes as they approached the Greek island. The German aircraft quickly flew out of sight, however. A few more sweeps followed before No 213 Sqn ceased flying from North Africa pending a move to Italy.

A few weeks earlier No 260 Sqn at Cutella, in Italy, had received a few Mustang Is as trainers prior to the unit replacing its Kittyhawk IIIs

The first unit to receive Mustang IIIs in Italy was No 260 Sqn, and amongst its aircraft was FB254/HS-J that was christened *Jovial Judge* by its unknown pilot. The fighter had the original framed cockpit cover. No 260 Sqn saw little action against enemy aircraft with the Mustang III (*R Thomas*)

The Mustang III squadrons supporting the fighting in Italy belonged to No 239 Wing, which had experienced South African ace Lt Col Laurie Wilmot (right) as its leader during the summer of 1944. Here, he is seen in conversation with Flt Lt Ken Richards, who later flew Mustang IIIs with No 3 Sqn RAAF (*author's collection*)

Like most wing leaders, Wilmot adorned his personal aircraft – in this case FB260 – with his initials. Here, they have been applied in a more decorative form. This fighter also carries a wing commander's rank pennant beneath the cockpit (*ww2images*)

with Mustang IIIs within No 239 Wing. The latter was led by distinguished South African ace Lt Col Laurie Wilmot, who soon acquired a personally marked Mustang III. No 260 then became established at San Angelo, to the north of Naples, where it supported the Allied drive north from Rome.

At the end of June No 112 Sqn also began to re-equip with Mustang IIIs, the unit commencing operations on 5 July. However, by now little was seen of the Luftwaffe in Italy, whilst the Aeronautica Nazionale Repubblicana (ANR) of the Italian Fascist state was mainly based in the north of Italy.

On the east coast on 1 July the Balkan Air Force (BAF) formed to co-ordinate air operations over the Adriatic and the Balkans. No 213 Sqn eventually moved into Biferno, on the east coast near Termoli, from where it began operations in mid-July as part of No 254 Wing. There remained, however, significant enemy air strength in Yugoslavia, including fighters and ground attack aircraft, so there were going to be some, albeit limited, opportunities for air combat, although the focus was on ground attack and interdiction work. The latter was the main task for the BAF units in Yugoslavia and Greece to disrupt enemy movement and eventual withdrawal.

Nevertheless, No 213 Sqn soon began adding to its impressive score sheet with the Mustang III when it began flying sorties against a German offensive that was pressurising the Partisans in Montenegro. On 15 July, in spite of bad weather over Yugoslavia, further sorties were launched. Soon after 0700 hrs the CO (in FB337) led Flg Off Anthony and WOs Cooke and Ford on a sweep that took them along a railway line that ran the length of the Serbian-Croatian border. Having strafed two trains, the pilots then spotted six single-engined biplanes, thought to

have been Bucker trainers, near the Croatian town of Vukovar. In a brief one-sided action, four of them were shot down, two falling to Spencer Whiting and one each to Anthony and Cooke. They then flew on. Eventually climbing to 9000 ft, the quartet headed for Sarajevo, where at 0915 hrs they spotted several aircraft on an airfield and two 'Dorniers' were attacked and set on fire before the Mustang III pilots set course for home.

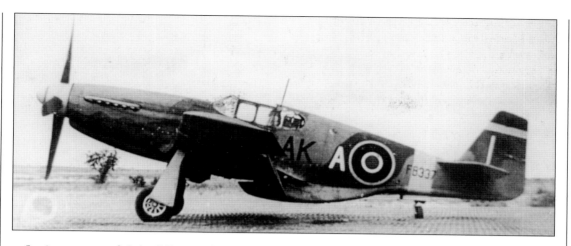

Sarajeveo was strafed the following day too, and a pair of biplanes destroyed. A Ju 52/3m was also destroyed on the ground at Shijak. There were further sweeps over the next few days, with 20 July proving to be the most intense day in terms of action since the unit had arrived in Italy. Missions were flown from dawn to dusk, with No 213 Sqn's operational record book describing the unit's most successful air combat with the Mustang III in the following terms;

'At 1115 hrs four Mustangs set out on an offensive sweep of roads from Beran-Mitrovi-Marina. In the Rozaj area the Mustangs flew into 12 Hs 126s, with an escort of seven Me 109s. In the ensuing engagement the Mustangs attacked from below and astern and the '109s seemed eager to break away after four or five minutes. The '109s seemed to be carrying either underslung long range fuselage tanks or bombs. which they did not attempt to jettison. Sqn Ldr Whiting claimed one Me 109G destroyed and one probable; WO Cooke claimed a probable and WO Watkins two Me 109Gs damaged.

'The Sections then separated, and at 1205 hrs the CO and WO Cooke met up again with the Hs 126s flying in four unescorted vics. The rear vic was attacked, the CO claiming one Hs126 destroyed and one damaged. WO Cooke claimed two damaged. The weather was fair but eight-tenths cloud at 8500 ft gave the enemy fighters good cover.'

These victories (claimed in FB337) took Spencer Whiting's total to four destroyed in just a few days, but unfortunately for him the opportunity to add his fifth never came. Further attacks on airfields were tasked in the last week of July following reports of considerable German air activity, several aircraft being strafed on the ground on the 27th when Whiting's fire left a Ju 52/3m burning at Nis.

Four days later No 213 Sqn flight commander Flt Lt Scott Vos (in FB328), who was regarded as the unit's 'ace' navigator, could do nothing to find his target in the Stygian gloom he found over Yugoslavia. However, returning over the Gulf of Fiume near Otocae, with 2Lt Pienaar on his wing, he found a three-engined Savoia-Marchetti SM.79 that they immediately attacked and shot down, Pienaar commenting on landing that 'it was all over far too quickly – after one burst it exploded in flames and crashed into the sea'. Sadly, Pienaar was killed on 4 August, and Scott Vos was also shot down on the 26th of that same month

Although No 213 Sqn produced no aces on the Mustang III, it did have an 'ace' aircraft! FB337/AK-A was the regular mount of Sqn Ldr Spencer Whiting, who in two combats at its controls over Yugoslavia claimed four destroyed, while Lt Ron Rorvik scored one of his four victories in it and Flt Sgt David Firman got two (*S R Whiting via Steve Brooking*)

when the squadron was conducting anti-flak sorties. He was rescued by partisans and had returned to his unit by the end of August.

Soon after this No 213 Sqn joined No 283 Wing, and through September the pace of operations increased as the enemy's position in Greece and the Balkans became more perilous, prompting withdrawals following the collapse on the Eastern Front. The wing CO was Grp Capt D S MacDonald, who had gained three victories flying with No 213 Sqn earlier in the war, and who on 5 September led an armed reconnaissance along the River Danube.

No 213 Sqn produced no aces on the Mustang III, but four of its pilots claimed four victories, including this trio, Flt Lt 'Tigger' Smith, Sqn Ldr Spencer Whiting and Flt Lt Scott Vos. By this stage of the war most squadrons in the RAF were very cosmopolitan in their make up – Smith originated from Trinidad whilst the other two hailed from South Africa! (*No 213 Sqn Records*)

The following day another patrol near the Serbian town of Sombor spotted a formation of four Bf 110s that had just taken off. Closing quickly from behind, and enjoying complete surprise, the No 213 Sqn pilots quickly shot three of them down. Flt Lt C D A Smith (in FB303) shared one with Lt Vorster, while Flt Sgt D E Firman (in FB308) also shot one down, as did WO S G Pickford (in HB894). The latter's victim was so well camouflaged that he had difficulty picking it out against the ground, becoming aware of the Bf 110 when he was almost wingtip-to-wingtip with its wingman! Although he had made five claims already, this was 'Tigger' Smith's first confirmed kill, and he too was to achieve four victories on the Mustang III – one of four No 213 Sqn pilots to do so!

There was more air action on the 7th when Lt R E Rorvik (in HB894) of the SAAF downed an Hs 126 over the Danube south of Sichevita. He had spotted it at 6000 ft, and with a short but devastating burst of gunfire sent it crashing into the river bank. This too was the first of his five claims that included four destroyed. More action came the next day during a sweep led by 'Tigger' Smith (in FB303) that also included Lts Vorster, Moore and Rorvik. Over Belgrade they attacked a Ju 52/3m, then spotted two He 111s each towing a Go 242 glider. Smith shot one He 111 down into the Danube, which was followed by the other Heinkel, while Rorvik (in HB894) shared in the destruction of one of the Go 242s. The other glider cast off and landed, whereupon it was destroyed by strafing.

On 9 September Sqn Ldr Whiting completed his third operational tour, for which he later received a well-deserved DSO. The squadron's purple patch continued the following day when Smith (in FB303) shot down another Ju 52/3m in flames east of Devdelija, in Greek Macedonia. A little while later, after a long chase, he also shared in the destruction of an He 111 with Ron Rorvik (in FB337). However, Sgt Brierley was thought to have been hit by return fire and was lost. It was the turn of Scott Vos (in HB902), perhaps celebrating his imminent promotion to command the squadron, to claim on 11 September when he shared a Ju 52/3m southwest of Dilfran with Flg Off Penson – the tri-motor transport crashed into a hillside.

Later that same day, during another sweep near Belgrade, Flt Lt J H Fairbairn (in HB854) also bagged one which fell near Uzdin while Sgt Bell shot down an Hs 126. The action continued the next day when Flt Lt Garwood severely damaged a Do 17 as it was landing at Pacevo, to the north of Belgrade, while Flt Sgt Firman damaged a Ju 88 and probably destroyed a Do 17 on the airfield.

Earlier in the month No 249 Sqn, under Sqn Ldr Jack te Kloot, began converting to the Mustang III, moving to Canne on the east coast of Italy to operate alongside No 213 Sqn. After some initial scepticism at having to give up their Spitfire IXs, the pilots' views on the American fighter soon changed as the rugged and elegant Mustang IIIs could hit targets anywhere in the Balkans. 'A' Flight converted first, followed by 'B' Flight, and the whole unit was operational within two weeks. It flew its first operation on 13 September when the CO and 2Lt Shields made a sweep along the Vardar valley into northern Greece, shooting up some locomotives. The pair flew another operation that afternoon, although when attacking a large motorised transport convoy Shields was hit and forced to bail out. Luckily he was picked up by Partisans and got back to Italy in late October.

That same day, pressing on with a sweep in poor weather, Flt Lt John Fairbairn (in HB888) led a section from No 213 Sqn to the Belgrade area, and north of Crepoja he probably destroyed an SM.79. During the attack his wingtip hit an obstruction and he crashed, surviving with a broken leg to become a PoW. On 17 September Sqn Ldr te Kloot led 15 aircraft, which included two sections from No 213 Sqn, on a sweep of the Prilep area. A Bulgarian Do 217 was seen near in the target area, and a section from No 213 Sqn was ordered to attack it. Lt Rorvik (in FB337) claimed the bomber probably destroyed to the northeast of Lake Ohrid, as when he last saw the aircraft it was diving steeply with an engine on fire. It was

On 21 September 1944, a quartet of Mustang IIIs from the recently equipped No 249 Sqn flew to a landing ground dubbed 'Piccadilly Peggy' in northern Greece that had been prepared by Partisans. Here, appropriately attired in his bush hat, Sqn Ldr Jack te Kloot (the unit's Australian CO) supervises the bedding down of his aircraft at 'Piccadilly Peggy' by the local partisans (*J te Kloot*)

the start of a busy and successful two weeks for the wing, and particularly for No 249 Sqn's Australian CO.

Early on the morning of 21 September a pair of Mustang IIIs from No 249 attacked Larissa, where Flg Off Ashworth and Sgt Manning each destroyed a Ju 52/3m. The latter, however, flew through a hail of light flak and took a number of hits, compelling him to bail out. Manning too was aided by Partisans, and he was soon back in Italy. That same day, during a sweep over Albania, No 213 Sqn's 'Pickles' Pickford (in HB854) encountered some Bf 109s that had just taken off from Tirana, and he shot one down and damaged a second. Later that afternoon, Jack te Kloot led three other Mustang IIIs to a secret airstrip prepared for the unit by Partisans in the mountains of northern Greece.

The Germans were evacuating Greece up the Vardar River valley, and the detachment was to mount further attacks on retreating Wehrmacht. At first light te Kloot led his pair off, and they carried out a number of strafing attacks on enemy transport across Salonika, before targeting an enemy landing strip at Megara. Diving down, he destroyed two Ju 52/3m transports parked here, before moving on and strafing a military parade. Upon his return to Brindisi, te Kloot noted;

'Two Ju 52s destroyed on Megara landing ground near Athens, two locos destroyed and three damaged, several oil wagons fired, three motorised transports destroyed and one damaged, one bullshit parade liquidated.'

However, the other pair of fighters that also sortied failed to return, Flt Lt Alf Dryden being killed after being struck by debris from an exploding train and Capt Whittingham bailing out when his Mustang III was hit by flak – the latter returned to the unit that night. This was the first of a number of attacks mounted from the strip, codenamed 'Piccadilly Peggy'. Early on the 23rd te Kloot led 2Lt J Malherbe on a further series of attacks against enemy communications, before heading for Tatoi airfield, near Athens. At the latter site the pair found 20+ Ju 52/3ms parked on the ground, as well as some Bf 109s in pens in the northwest corner of the airfield. Sweeping in at low-level, the pair destroyed five of the transports, three being credited to te Kloot, before they returned north to attack further rail stock.

Also seen at 'Piccadilly Peggy', HB946/GN-E is being camouflaged for the night by the locals. It was flown from this location on a successful strafing mission by 2Lt Malherbe on 23 September, the SAAF pilot destroying two Ju 52/3ms (*J te Kloot*)

Bad weather then intervened and No 249 Sqn's Mustang IIIs were not seen back over Greece again until 27 September, when four hit further rail transport and then strafed Prokhama airfield. Flg Off Doug McCaig, who hailed from Fiji, recounted this typical attack many years later;

'Squeezing down the tension, I checked the guns to fire, gunsight on. I saw them in the blink of an eye, a perfect blue silhouette, a Focke-Wulf Fw 190 – I couldn't believe it. The second, just behind, showed the tailplane and cockpit canopy. Squeezing the trigger exploded my 0.5s in a spray, all four guns roaring. The nearest one was smouldering, the second took my bursts, leaping and jumping all over its engine cowling and cockpit. A whole world of armament was coming up at us, lines of arcing tracer, vicious, bright in the shrouded light.'

McCaig was credited with both aircraft probably destroyed, while Flt Sgt Davey destroyed a third. One of the other pair was lost to ground fire, however, for despite their parlous situation, German flak was as efficient and deadly as ever. The following day Sqn Ldr te Kloot led Flt Lt Noble on another highly profitable attack on Salonika airfield, as the former noted in his flying logbook;

'Strafed main aerodrome at Salonika – one Ju 52 destroyed, one "Iti" destroyed, one He 111 destroyed, one Go 242 glider damaged. Flt Lt Noble three enemy aircraft damaged.'

They then attacked further targets, where the CO had a lucky escape, as he noted again;

'Four locos destroyed, two damaged. Received 40 mm cannon shell in wing. Aircraft write-off on return to base.'

In a very successful week Jack te Kloot had personally destroyed eight enemy aircraft on the ground and damaged a ninth. Both Nos 213 and 249 Sqns continued to take a heavy toll of the enemy forces as they withdrew from the Balkans, but in return both units too had taken a steady stream of losses, although many pilots were picked up by the Partisans and eventually returned to Italy.

THE LAST VICTORIES

In Italy the long, grinding advance had continued, with both Nos 260 and 112 Sqns flying countless ground attacks in support of Allied troops.

The distinctive 'sharksmouth' markings readily identify this aircraft of No 112 Sqn in Italy during the summer of 1944. What is less apparent is that it is thought to be HB936/GA-A, which was the aircraft in which Sgt Arthur Banks, later awarded the George Cross for his gallantry, was shot down (*via R L Ward*)

Like the squadrons flying over Yugoslavia, they too suffered depressingly heavy losses as the British Army conducted what was described by one general as 'some of the bloodiest fighting' of the entire war.

Taking part in No 112 Sqn's third operation of 29 August was Sgt Arthur Banks, who was flying HB936/GA-A. Between Ravenna and Ferrara his fighter was hit by flak and he force-landed. Behind enemy lines the young Welshman managed to join a partisan group, and he remained with them organising their activities until when trying to cross to Allied territory in early December he was captured. Handed over to the SS and Italian Fascists, Banks was tortured and eventually killed. The citation for his posthumous award of the George Cross stated, 'His conduct was at all times in keeping with the highest traditions of the service, even in the face of brutal and inhuman treatment.'

One of the unit's most successful days flying the Mustang III was 9 September when, led by CO Sqn Ldr A P Q Bluett, 11 fighters bombed a 200-ton vessel near Trieste and left it listing and beached, before attacking barges in the harbour and also strafing some trains. Rivolto airfield was then strafed, and two Re.2001s and two Bf 109s were left damaged as the unit moved on to nearby Aviano, where six SM.79s were attacked and four destroyed. A pair of fighters that had become separated from the main force also attacked an He 111 on another airfield and left that wrecked too.

That evening, another armed reconnaissance was led by Flt Lt Ray Hearn that saw a railway yard at Cesena attacked before the pilots strafed an airfield, leaving three SM.79s wrecked and burning. They then moved on to Vicenza, where a Ju 52/3m was destroyed on the ground. Shortly afterwards Hearn sighted what he reported as a Ju 88 flying very low. Closing in, and with just one gun firing, he gained hits on the starboard engine, causing the bomber to turn and crash on the airfield in a cloud of dust. He had just claimed what records show was No 112 Sqn's 198th, and final, victory. His victim was in fact an Me 410 of 2.(F)/122, and it had become No 112 Sqn's only kill with the Mustang III.

Although there was little to be seen of enemy aircraft over Italy, the skies over Yugoslavia still produced the occasional combat. On 10 October No 213 Sqn's CO, Sqn Ldr Scott Vos (in HB902), led a section that encountered two unidentified aircraft that were shot down, the shared victories taking his total to four destroyed and one damaged. Although identified as 'Fieselers', they may have been Croatian Bucker

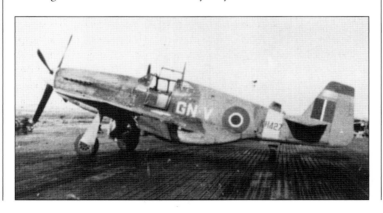

Sqn Ldr Jack te Kloot flew the final mission of his tour as CO of No 249 Sqn in HB427/GN-V on 2 December 1944 when he led an attack on a road bridge near Bioce. More significantly, the fighter had also been flown by Flt Lt R F Noble when he had shared in the destruction of the last aircraft claimed by the squadron on 31 October (*J te Kloot*)

Bu 131s – Flt Sgt Firman (in FB337) also claimed a share in both kills. No 213 Sqn's diary entry for 15 October described a further encounter;

'Offensive sweep against enemy aircraft over Zagreb-Sisak area. Sighted CR.42 at 1000 ft flying west towards Sisak on parallel course, three miles to starboard. Attacked by Sgt Hunt and Flg Off Allan, and strikes observed. Enemy aircraft crash-landed and pilot seen to leave it in a position one mile north of river and eight miles southeast of Sisak. CR.42 not destroyed so strafed and set on fire.'

There was another success on the 21st during another sweep when four of them came across a Croatian Fi 167 reconnaissance bomber flying to the southwest of Binj. It duly crashed and burst into flames after being attacked by all four Mustang IIIs. One of the pilots involved was Lt Ron Rorvik (in FB303), who thus claimed his fourth success. Sadly, he crashed in bad weather at the end of the month and was killed.

On the 30th Grp Capt MacDonald led four Mustangs from No 213 Sqn and three from No 249 Sqn on an offensive sweep over southern Yugoslavia up towards Skopje where, over the mountains, they hit heavy cloud and very bad weather. Although some of the pilots managed to descend and attack transport targets, weather such as this soon became depressingly familiar throughout the winter months.

The following day two more Mustang IIIs from No 249 Sqn, flown by Flt Lt P F Noble and Flg Off John Dickerson, conducted an armed reconnaissance over Albania. North of Bitol they spotted an Fi 156 Storch flying at low-level, as Dickerson recalled;

'Flt Lt Noble, who was at least 1000 yards ahead of me, fired on the Storch, which was flying very low, although I didn't see his rounds as we didn't use tracer ammunition – the effects of the ricochets when attacking ground targets was rather alarming. I followed in from a different angle, and remember feeling surprised at how like the official Aircraft Recognition cards the Storch looked!

'The pilot didn't seem to realise he was being attacked, as he was turning gently to port. I was closing very rapidly on him and managed to get in a brief, optimistic, burst of fire at a narrow deflection angle, without obvious results, before overshooting and pulling round sharply to avoid the wooded valley side. As I came round I looked back and saw that the Storch had struck the hillside. There was no fire or explosion, and the wings were folded back over a bent fuselage.'

This kill took the squadron's total claims to 328.5, making it one of the top-scoring RAF squadrons of the war.

Another unit had also begun to re-equip with Mustang IIIs in late September, No 5 Sqn SAAF flying its first operations with the new type on 5 October from Iesi, near Ancona on the Adriatic coast. On that date the unit strafed some motorised transports near Rimini. In addition to missions over Italy, No 5 SAAF also regularly sortied over Yugoslavia too. November was, as its diary noted, 'an eventful month for No 5 Sqn'. On the 4th Lt Conrad Begg (in KH456) claimed the unit's first victory with the Mustang III while flying with five others on an armed reconnaissance of the Brod-Sarajevo railway line. Sighting a Ju 52/3m, Begg shot it down in flames, as he later described in his Combat Report;

'An aircraft, which was identified as a Ju 52, was sighted flying east to west at "angels 6". The leader closed in and saw the black crosses. The

Ju 52 then opened fire, but as the leader had to lay off deflection I closed in and made a fine quarter attack from above, opening fire at a range of about 150 yards and closing in to about 50 yards. After my first burst the port engine and inner wing caught fire. This spread to the fuselage. The aircraft lost height, burning fiercely, and was followed down by the rest of the flight. It crashed in a nearby field.'

Five days later Begg (in KH487) was on a weather reconnaissance to the south of Zagreb when he came across another of the lumbering transports;

'I sighted a Ju 52 and flew alongside it, at which point I saw the black crosses. The aircraft opened fire on me and I was hit in the wing and tail. I broke away, jettisoned my long range tanks and attacked the aircraft from astern as it was diving into a rainstorm. I opened fire at about 400 yards and closed to about 200 yards, by which point both the fuselage and starboard engine had caught fire. The Ju 52 broke up in the air and crashed on the side of a mountain.'

It was the squadron's 71st, and last, victory of the war. During the month Capt 'Nobby' Clarke, who had three victories when flying Kittyhawks, was posted in as flight commander.

—— 'SLEDGEHAMMERS FOR WALNUTS' ——

The sixth squadron to become operational in Italy also began conversion in mid-November when the first Mustang IIIs for the veteran No 3 Sqn Royal Australian Air Force (RAAF) arrived at Fano. It flew its first operation with the new aircraft on the 22nd when Sqn Ldr Murray Nash led an escort for a lone Lysander over northern Italy. The 'spy dropper' was downed by a USAAF P-51, however! The next operation came on the 25th when Flt Lt Roediger led a weather reconnaissance to the Ljubljana area of Yugoslavia, although this operation proved to be far less eventful.

Ground fire claimed another successful pilot in early December when Lt Conrad Begg was shot down and killed over Yugoslavia, his death coming after No 5 Sqn SAAF had lost eight pilots to flak during November alone.

No 3 Sqn RAAF re-equipped with Mustangs in the autumn of 1944. It had both Mk IIIs and IVs for a time, one of the latter being KH716/CV-P in which the CO, Sqn Ldr Nash, damaged a Bf 109 on Boxing Day 1944 (*F F Smith*)

No 3 Sqn RAAF only claimed two victories with the Mustang III/IV, the first of which was claimed by Flg Off 'Dusty' Lane, who had previously claimed two victories while flying Spitfire IXs with No 111 Sqn in 1944 *(RAAF)*

On the afternoon of 26 December enemy aircraft were encountered over northern Italy by No 3 Sqn RAAF for the first time since the unit had transitioned to the Mustang III, as Sqn Ldr Nash (in KH716) recalled;

'Plt Off Caldecott saw an aircraft, which was later identified as an ME 109, make an attack on WO Quinn, who was lagging behind the formation. The Mustangs then patrolled in the vicinity of Aviano in the hope of catching enemy aircraft on their return, and they were rewarded. Andrews, Thomas and I each got a burst in, and I saw hits as it came into land, though it was not seen to crash.'

Their claim was thus for a probable only, although the aircraft from the Italian Fascist ANR did in fact crash-land, as the pilot, who was named Squassoni, told Nash many years after the war!

Some of the units also began to receive examples of the 'bubble' hooded Mustang IV at this point, and the New Year opened for all the squadrons with the continued routine of bombing and armed reconnaissance flights over both northern Italy and Yugoslavia. Much motorised transport and rolling stock was claimed destroyed, with sorties often being flown in the face of dreadful weather and continued losses. On 18 February, for example, Flt Lt Ray Hearn (who had claimed No 112 Sqn's final victory) was shot down and killed by light flak while strafing Aviano airfield.

On 21 March No 3 Sqn RAAF flew in the anti-flak role for the No 239 Wing attack on Venice harbour, and three days later Nos 213 and 249 Sqns combined in an attack on Gornje-Stupnik airfield. Many German aircraft had reportedly been sighted there, although most had already been evacuated by the time of the attack. There was still aerial activity to be had over Yugoslavia, however. On 2 April, No 3 Sqn RAAF's Flg Off A F 'Dusty' Lane (in KH755) was part of a section that had left Cervia at 0625 hrs for an armed reconnaissance over Yugoslavia, where they attacked trains and motorised transport. The unit's operational diary then recounted what happened;

'Three or four miles south of Maribor, when at 2000 ft, a Fieseler Storch was seen going southeast almost on the deck. Flg Off Lane went up

and made sure of the black crosses, and then came around and shot it up from astern. It made a good crash-landing and two occupants got out and hid underneath the wings. Flg Off Lane and Flt Lt Edmonds each made a run or two, eventually setting the aircraft on fire and the bods ran away.'

This was Lane's third and final victory, and No 3 Sqn RAAF's first with the Mustang III/IV. The second was not long in coming, for the following afternoon Flt Lt A F Shannon led an eight aircraft formation for an armed reconnaissance of the Ljubljana-Maribor area, where another Fi 156 was encountered. The unit's diary recalled;

'Southeast of Maribor a Storch was seen going south at 50 ft. "Red 1" and "2" jettisoned their bombs and Flt Lt Shannon caught up with the aircraft, making a full beam attack from starboard (using bags of flap). He hit it in the engine and cockpit and it started to pour smoke and finally crashed in flames.'

No 3 Sqn RAAF's final victory was also the last to be credited to RAF and Commonwealth squadrons in the Mediterranean, the unit diary noting dryly, 'Talk about a sledgehammer for a walnut!'

In early April No 213 Sqn gained an experienced new flight commander in the form of Flt Lt 'Ginger' Hulse, who began a second tour of operations. He already had six claims, though he too had yet to gain a single confirmed victory – post-war research was to show that some of his claims had in fact crashed. Hulse flew his first operation on the 13th, when he led an armed reconnaissance that saw a railway bridge bombed and motorised transport strafed. The following day 'Nobby' Clarke became CO of No 5 Sqn SAAF as the war in Italy and the Balkans slowly drew to its conclusion.

The last of No 3 Sqn RAAF's many victories during the war fell to Flt Lt A F Shannon on 3 April 1945 when he was at the controls of KH794/CV-G (*F F Smith*)

The only SAAF unit to become operational on the Mustang was No 5 Sqn, to which KH681/GL-Z belonged. This aircraft was occasionally flown by one of its more successful pilots, Capt 'Nobby' Clarke, but it was shot down attacking a bridge in February 1945, killing pilot Capt P G Maguire (*SAAF*)

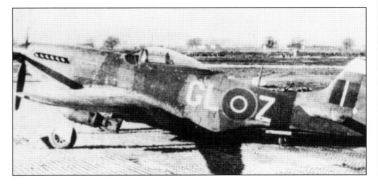

THUNDERBOLTS OVER BURMA

The second American single-engined fighter that enjoyed great success over Europe was the Republic P-47 Thunderbolt. Powered by a massive 2300 hp Pratt & Whitney Double Wasp R-2800 radial engine, Alexander Kartveli's design had an empty weight of 10,000 lbs – almost twice that of a loaded Spitfire – and although christened Thunderbolt, on entering service with the USAAF it was nicknamed 'Juggernaut', or 'Jug' for short. The P-47 began operations with the USAAF on long-range bomber escort missions in the spring of 1943, and fitted with external tanks, it would eventually fly deep into Germany.

The new US fighter had naturally attracted the attention of the RAF, but its initial deficiencies and the adequate provision of other types led to a lapse in interest. However, RAF squadrons based in India required a replacement for their Hurricanes to support planned operations to recapture Burma in 1944, and the Thunderbolt's range, ruggedness and firepower once more brought it into focus. Air Force HQ India therefore proposed that eight squadrons be re-equipped with the big American fighter in the long-range ground attack role, although doubts as to its suitability remained despite USAAF P-47Ds sometimes being used in this role in Europe!

Nevertheless, negotiations began for the supply of the P-47 to the RAF, and in January 1944 an agreement for the initial delivery of 420 examples and, incidentally, 300 Mustangs, was concluded. A monthly delivery

By the time RAF Thunderbolts were fully operational, the JAAF had almost been swept from the skies of Burma, so pilots flying the type only claimed a handful of victories. It was No 30 Sqn that earned the distinction of being the first to claim a Thunderbolt kill in the RAF, and this aircraft was one of the Mk IIs assigned to the unit – KJ131/RS-Y, which was usually flown by Flt Lt David Dick (*David Dick*)

allocation of 60 aircraft would permit training and attrition, and it was estimated that this would suffice for the formation of eight RAF squadrons with what was now officially designated the Thunderbolt. Although all deliveries were of P-47D sub-variants, the early 'razorbacked' aircraft was designated the Mk I and the later 'bubble-hood' fitted aircraft became the Mk II. Eventually 240 Mk Is and 590 Mk IIs were delivered. Two aircraft were also despatched to the UK for testing and service evaluation in March 1944, and a few others went to Karachi for in-theatre trials.

By mid-1944, with the tide turning in favour of the Allies in Assam around Imphal, the flow of Thunderbolts into India quickened. Hurricane units now began converting, with No 135 Sqn receiving its first examples in May. Its transition was overseen by No 1670 Conversion Unit at Yelahanka, where Nos 146 and 261 Sqns began their training in June, followed soon afterwards by Nos 79 and 30 Sqns and, finally, Nos 5, 123 and 258 Sqns in September.

No 30 Sqn began flying the big fighter on 15 July, Flt Lt D A McDonald recalling;

'The aircraft was a delight to fly, as it had a big spacious cockpit and controls that handled very well. I found that you had to help the Thunderbolt to get airborne, however.'

The RAF's biggest single-seat fighter of World War 2 finally began operations on 14 September when No 261 Sqn (which had moved up to Kumbhirigram, some 50 miles east of Imphal) mounted an armed reconnaissance over the Chindwin. Two days later it flew the RAF's first bombing sorties when six 500-lb bombs were dropped near Mawlaik. That same day sister unit No 146 Sqn also commenced Thunderbolt operations, strafing numerous targets around Imphal, Kalewa and Mawlaik.

By early October, with the weather steadily improving, the XIVth Army around Imphal began a four-pronged drive towards Homalin that was be dependent on air support. Further south, early October saw No 30 Sqn join No 135 Sqn in No 902 Wing and begin operations, the latter unit initially flying strafing missions with eight aircraft. No 30 Sqn also flew 'Rhubarbs' in support of the West Africans clearing the Arakan coast.

Another squadron to claim a Japanese victim was No 135 Sqn, which was commanded by Sqn Ldr Lee Hawkins. He had previously made five claims, including two destroyed, flying Hurricanes over Burma with the unit in March 1943 (*L C C Hawkins*)

Another unit active on escort duties was No 261 Sqn, whose CO, Sqn Ldr R H Fletcher, is seen here flying KL849/FJ-G in 1945 (*S Sakalas*)

No 135 Sqn was led by successful pilot Sqn Ldr Lee Hawkins, who had made five claims over Burma, and who on 18 October led his first Thunderbolt mission. In another one two days later, a large number of Japanese troops were killed when six Thunderbolts attacked them in the Kaladan River area.

Bombing and strafing ground attacks soon became the RAF Thunderbolt's staple task. From Chittagong, both squadrons were also soon providing escorts for Liberator bombing raids and vital Dakota transport missions, and these were to ultimately result in a few brief skirmishes with the Japanese Army Air Force (JAAF).

At the same time Nos 146 and 261 Sqns moved down to Cox's Bazaar on the coast so as to operate alongside the USAAF's 1st Air Commando Group on a special long-range mission to the Rangoon area. It was estimated that the attack could be opposed by up to 50 JAAF aircraft, but in the event the RAF Thunderbolts saw nothing over their target at Zayatkwin. However, on 20 October a further big fighter sweep again included these units, which targeted Mingaladon, as the enemy had flown in reinforcements – including some of the 50th Sentai's new Ki-84 Hayate ('Frank') fighters.

Over the target the Thunderbolts found those JAAF aircraft that had scrambled flying in a huge defensive circle that made successful attacks difficult. However, Plt Off R C Rees (in HD183) of No 261 Sqn did attack a Ki-61 'Tony' and may have caused damage to it, while squadronmate WO Carter (in HD185) spotted some aircraft at the end of the runway and diving down after them, claiming a Ki-44 'Tojo' probably destroyed. After this both Thunderbolt squadrons returned north to Kumbhirgram, where at the end of the month they were joined in No 909 Wing by No 79 Sqn, under the command of Sqn Ldr 'Gritty' Humphries.

Toward the end of October No 30 Sqn's first Mk IIs arrived, and they were fitted with long-range tanks so that they could be used for bomber escort work. Soon afterwards the No 902 Wing squadrons moved down the coast to Cox's Bazaar for Operation *Eruption*, and the units flew their first mission on 3 November with a sweep over the Rangoon airfields in support of a bombing raid by 49 USAAF B-29s and 28 B-24s on the

This photograph of No 135 Sqn Thunderbolt Is was taken at Chittagong in late 1944. The nearest aircraft is HD173/A and next to it is HB982/D, which was being flown by Plt Off Bob Windle on 17 November when he shared in the destruction of a Ki-43 over Rangoon (*via G J Thomas*)

city's important railway marshalling yards. No 30's aircraft lifted off at 0730 hrs, and in fine weather No 135 Sqn swept over Mingaladon. Three Ki-43 'Oscars' were seen but they did not attempt to interfere with the attack. WO Wright of No 30 Sqn, who had taken off late, then arrived and closed on three aircraft he thought were Thunderbolts. It was only when he was much closer to them that he spotted their unusual camouflage and blood red roundels! Wright fired on one, and as another closed on his tail he beat a discretionary retreat into nearby cloud!

The Insein railway workshops were the target for a large formation of Liberators the next day, their escort including the Thunderbolts of Nos 30 and 135 Sqns. After the 'heavies' had bombed, the formation was attacked by a mix of Ki-43 'Oscars' and Ki-44 'Tojo' fighters. Flying HD289/RS-S, Flt Lt Harry Whidborne attacked one of the Ki-44s, seeing hits on the cockpit area and causing it to burn. Flt Lt Fulford (in HD208) then fired on the same aircraft and it fell away in flames, its destruction being witnessed by a USAAF P-38 pilot. The RAF's Thunderbolt units had at last scored their first success!

Flt Lt Harry Whidborne of No 30 Sqn shared in the shooting down of a Ki-44 over Rangoon on 3 November 1944, this aircraft representing the first victory claim made by RAF Thunderbolts (*via J Hamlin*)

The squadrons further north also remained active, and on 11 November nine aircraft from No 146 Sqn attacked Meiktila and Thedaw airfields. At the latter WO Cope destroyed a single-engined aircraft on the ground. Two more were then seen taxiing and one of these was probably destroyed by Flt Lt Ivens, although on the debit side WO Griffiths was hit by ground fire and force-landed to become a PoW. Then on 17 November two-dozen aircraft from Nos 30 and 135 Sqns again escorted Liberators to Rangoon, and the formation was intercepted by around 20 Ki-43s and Ki-44s as it approached the target. Flt Sgt R E Maxwell and Plt Off Bob Windle from No 135 Sqn engaged a 50th Sentai Ki-43 as it attempted to intercept the bombers, hitting it and forcing Sgt Shinohara to bail out. Then near Hmawbi WO Evans of No 30 Sqn and No 135 Sqn's Flt Sgt Hammond each damaged a Ki-43. Although the pilots involved did not know it at the time, this was to prove to be the Thunderbolt's most successful air action in RAF service.

On both the 19th and 23rd these two squadrons again provided escort to bombers attacking the railways around Rangoon, and although there were brief encounters, they could make no claims against the nimble JAAF fighters.

At this time Nos 79, 146 and 261 Sqns moved east with No 910 Wing to Wangjing, 15 miles south of Imphal, as the XIVth Army had become established across the Chindwin River and had started its advance into Burma. On 25 November 11 fighters from No 261 Sqn strafed Meiktila and Heho, and at the latter airfield WO Owen destroyed a Ki-46.

The following day more Thunderbolts arrived for operations when No 905 Wing at Ratnap, near Cox's Bazaar, received Nos 134 and 258 Sqns. The latter, flying a mix of nine 'razorback' Thunderbolt Is and seven bubble-hooded Mk IIs, was commanded by Sqn Ldr Neil Cameron, who had seven claims, including three and one shared victories from his varied service in the UK, Russia and the Middle East. The wing began operations on 7 December, and on the 12th No 258 Sqn flew a sweep over Magwe, dropping some 500-lb bombs.

The long-range attacks continued the attrition of the JAAF when, on the 10th, No 79 Sqn sent nine Thunderbolts to Thedaw, near Meiktila. There, Flg Off Craymer spotted an aircraft that he identified as a Ki-43 and attacked, causing it to blow up. It was in fact a Ki-36 'Ida' army co-operation aircraft, and Flg Off Reed claimed a second damaged, although this was later upgraded to destroyed.

The Thunderbolt squadrons continued escorting long-range bombing raids to southern Burma, such as on 13 December when Nos 30 and 135 Sqns protected Liberators sent to attack a railway bridge ahead of the advancing West African Division as it moved down the Kaladan Valley. The formation was attacked by Ki-43s from the 50th Sentai, and although some of the USAAF fighters made claims, success eluded the RAF units. Both squadrons provided escort to another attack by US B-24s the following day.

Nos 5 and 123 Sqns now also became operational on the Thunderbolt, moving into Nazir to join No 258 Sqn in support to the West African Division. In the main, however, the JAAF was absent and largely a spent force, although strafing attacks on airfields continued, such as on the last day of 1944 when Nos 79, 146 and 261 Sqns strafed Meiktila and Thedaw. Two Ki-43s were destroyed and two damaged.

In January 1945 the advance into Burma really began to make headway, with the Japanese 28th Army in the Arakan abandoning Akyab. This in turn allowed amphibious landings to be made at Myebon and

The only pilot to become an ace whilst flying an RAF Thunderbolt was No 258 Sqn's CO, Sqn Ldr Neil Cameron, who, when escorting Liberators over Rangoon on 11 February 1945, shared in the destruction of a Ki-61. It was his fifth success, Cameron having previously enjoyed success flying Hurricanes in the UK, Russia and the Middle East (*author's collection*)

When he achieved his fifth victory, Neil Cameron was flying Thunderbolt II HD292/ZT-L, and although of poor quality, this photograph is believed to have been taken from one of the Liberators during the very mission on which he claimed his fifth kill (*via G J Thomas*)

Ramree, thus putting further pressure on the enemy. On the 11th the battle for the Irrawaddy crossing began when the 19th Indian Division overcame the mighty river barrier and formed a strong bridgehead. However, with so few targets available, the No 224 Group Thunderbolt squadrons entered something of a brief hiatus, although on the 13th Sqn Ldr 'Gatty' May led No 79 Sqn on a sweep, and at Kangaung they spotted four Ki-43s that were duly strafed and claimed destroyed. Close support to the advancing troops was the priority of the Thunderbolt squadrons though, and opportunities to engage JAAF fighters in aerial combat became increasingly rare.

On 29 January No 123 Sqn escorted a USAAF raid, and as the formation turned for home several pairs of enemy fighters appeared, although only one ventured to attack. However, as Flt Lt Aris positioned to attack the Ki-43 half-rolled and dived away.

11 February saw the heaviest bombing raid thus far of the campaign in Burma, with storage dumps near Rangoon being the target for the 84 Liberators of the 7th BG and Nos 99, 215, 355 and 356 Sqns, and 59 USAAF B-29s. The 'heavies' were escorted by USAAF P-38s and the Thunderbolts of Nos 30, 134 and 258 Sqns, the latter led by Sqn Ldr Neil Cameron. Over the target six Ki-61s from the 8th Rensai Hikotai (a fighter operational training unit) attempted to intercept the raiders,

One of the RAF's leading aces, Grp Capt Frank Carey commanded No 73 OTU at Fayid, in Egypt, from late 1944. The unit was tasked with the training of Thunderbolt pilots (*via Norman Franks*)

one of them flying under the rear of the formation as the pilot tried to gain position for a beam attack. However, as it did so fire from several Liberator gunners poured into it. At the same time, Cameron, in his usual aircraft (HD292/ZT-L), attacked the 'Tony' head on, following which the pilot was seen to bail out. Aboard one of the No 356 Sqn Liberators, Flt Lt Frank Dismore described how;

'Jap fighters dropped aerial bombs and then sliced down to our level. Thunderbolts met them, and not one was able to concentrate on our squadron. Some of the "Libs" in front seemed to be troubled, for a Jap was shot down almost immediately. The pilot bailed out and floated by as we progressed.'

One of No 258 Sqn's pilots more succinctly recorded afterwards, 'In came the fighters and the bombers put out a terrific barrage, but Neil Cameron just went in and sawed the tail off a "Jack" (sic)'. Cameron initially only claimed the Ki-61 as a possible, as he thought that it might have been hit by the bombers' gunners, but he was credited with a half-share in its destruction with WO McCredie, a turret gunner from No 99 Sqn. In being elevated to acedom, Neil Cameron had also made the only claim by an ace when flying an RAF Thunderbolt – indeed, it was the type's final victory in British colours. Cameron went on to have a distinguished post-war career, rising to become Chief of the Air Staff –

At Fayid, Carey adopted Thunderbolt II KJ348 as his personal mount, having it painted black overall with a distinctive red stripe so that his students would better identify him when he was in the air (*F H Carey via Norman Franks*)

Most No 73 OTU Thunderbolts were camouflaged, but one natural metal example was KL328, which was often flown by the Chief Instructor, Sqn Ldr 'Nobby' Clarke. Like his CO, he was a notable pilot with a number of victories to his name (*Newark Air Museum*)

he was the last fighter ace to hold this position. His unique claim to fame as the only RAF pilot to become an ace while flying a Thunderbolt also virtually marked the end of the aircraft's career as an escort fighter in Burma. Thereafter, it flew solely on ground attack duties, which were conducted with distinction. Probably the last aircraft destroyed by the Thunderbolt in RAF service were a bomber and a Ki-44 that were strafed during a sweep to Moulmein at the end of April 1945.

EGYPTIAN TRAINING

In India, in addition to the Conversion Unit, some Thunderbolts were also flown at the Advanced Fighter Training Unit at Armada Road for tactical training. Amongst its staff were several successful pilots from the Burma campaign, including ace Flt Lt 'Banger' Yates. The main training organisation to fly the Thunderbolt was, however, No 73 Operational Training Unit (OTU) at Fayid, on the Suez Canal in Egypt. In early November 1944 one of the RAF's foremost fighter aces, Grp Capt Frank Carey, was posted in to command. He recalled;

'Being a major flying training station, it had lashings of aerial activity from many different two-seater trainers and fighter types. These included Spitfires, Harvards, Thunderbolts, Fairchilds and Masters. This OTU was to change its role to support the requirements of the Far East, and I was sent there temporarily to oversee these changes.'

At Fayid, he adopted Thunderbolt II KJ348 as his personal mount. It was in an all black colour scheme with a broad stripe down the fuselage to make Carey instantly recognisable when in the air. One of his instructors was Flt Lt F W T Davies, who had known him in Burma and who recalled this aircraft;

'Carey had a smart Thunderbolt II painted black with a red stripe down the sides on which he occasionally demonstrated his skill, despite the fighter weighing in at seven tons.'

The Chief Flying Instructor at No 73 OTU was a notable pilot from the desert war, Sqn Ldr D H 'Nobby' Clarke, who had five claims, including two and one shared destroyed. However, with the end of the war against Japan that summer, the OTU began to run down and the operational squadrons in the Far East, some of which saw brief post-war action against Indonesian rebels in Java, all disbanded soon afterwards.

VALEDICTION

From Italy, interdiction operations continued apace, with No 213 Sqn hitting the Yugoslav railways, and No 3 Sqn RAAF bombing numerous Italian river crossings ahead of the steadily advancing British Eighth Army, for example.

At midday on 23 April 1945 Flt Lt Graham Hulse, flying his regular aircraft KH826/AK-G, and Flg Off Barrett were in the vicinity of Zagreb on an armed reconnaissance when they were bounced by a pair of Croatian Bf 109Gs. Barrett was hit by fire from the Croatian ace Capt Ljudevit Bencetic and he became the last of his 16 victories.

However, his wingman, Lt Mihajlo Jelak, flying Bf 109G-14 'Black 27', was then hit and badly damaged by Hulse, the Messerschmitt in fact crash-landing. The whole combat, which lasted some ten minutes, ended at treetop

The RAF's last aerial claim in the Mediterranean was made by Flt Lt 'Ginger' Hulse of No 213 Sqn who, in a combat with a pair of Croatian Bf 109s on 23 April 1945, claimed one of them damaged, although in fact it crash-landed (*I Simpson*)

By the spring of 1945, many of No 213 Sqn's Mustang IVs were uncamouflaged. The nearer one is KH797/AK-A and beyond it is KH826/AK-G, which was flown by Flt Lt Hulse in the final air combat of the air war in the Mediterranean (*No 213 Sqn Records*)

height, and is depicted on the cover of *Osprey Aircraft of the Aces 49 – Croatian Aces of World War 2.*

Graham Hulse described his seventh combat claim of World War 2 (he was to make a further four kill claims against MiG-15s flying F-86 Sabres with the USAF during the Korean War);

'Flying at 8000 ft from Zagreb to Bisak, my section was jumped by two ME 109s. that were blue/grey in camouflage, with yellow tails and spinners and black crosses. They attacked from above and behind. Flg Off Barratt called up to say he had been hit by a '109 in the port wingtip. ME 109s then broke down, and I attacked one from close range at 2000 ft. I followed my '109 down to the deck and fired several bursts, closing to 150 yards. I observed 10-15 strikes on its port wing and fuselage. Pieces of aircraft broke away in a cloud of black smoke. I then ran out of ammunition. Light flak was encountered over Zagreb 'drome so my attack had to be broken off. Flg Off Barratt hit by flak – missing. I claim one 1 ME 109 damaged.'

Hulse landed at Prkos 45 minutes later, having just made the very last claim by a Commonwealth fighter pilot in the Mediterranean theatre of operations. Ground attack missions continued, regardless, No 3 Sqn RAAF hitting some lock gates two days later.

However, secret negotiations had been ongoing and a document was signed instructing all German forces in Italy to surrender unconditionally to the Allies on 2 May.

In a tragic piece of irony, on 1 May the CO of No 5 Sqn SAAF, Maj 'Nobby' Clarke, was shot down by flak fired from a ship that he was attacking in Grado harbour during the unit's very last operation. Some operational reconnaissance missions continued to be flown for several days, Hulse, who was by then No 213 Sqn's acting CO, taking

This Mustang IV failed to return from the 4 May 1945 shipping strike off the Danish islands, Plt Off Peter Bell of No 234 Sqn being wounded by flak in KH860/AZ-G and force-landing in Denmark, where he briefly became a PoW (*R T Williams*)

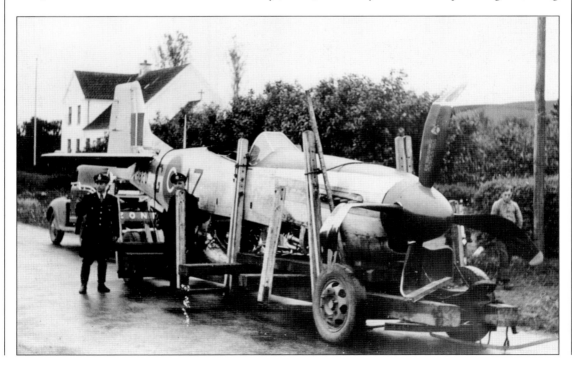

This photograph of Mustang III KH430/5J-A of No 126 Sqn was taken at Lüneburg on 4 May after it had landed there following the Danish islands shipping strike in which the squadron CO had so tragically been killed. Earlier, when with No 64 Sqn, this aircraft was flown by Flg Off Don Smiley, who on 16 January 1945 had used it to shoot down a Bf 109 over Frankfurt (*M Robinson*)

The last operational sorties flown by RAF Mustang III/IVs in the UK were undertaken as cover for the re-occupation of the Channel Islands, for which the Hunsdon Wing was led by Wg Cdr 'Jas' Storrar (*via C F Shores*)

off at 0715 hrs on 5 May for his last mission of the war, shortly before another section flew the unit's last operation of the war in Europe to the Ljubljana-Vransko area.

Back in Britain, the Mustang III/IV squadrons based in Scotland and eastern England continued to fly off the Danish and Norwegian coasts, escorting coastal strike missions. The day of the enemy surrender in Italy, 2 May, Wg Cdr Peter Wickham led an escort to the Kattegat for 22 Mosquitos, which attacked two U-boats. The following day Bentwaters Wing leader Wg Cdr Kaj Birksted led an escort that included Nos 118 and 234 Sqns on a shipping strike off Denmark.

The last sorties came on 4 May, and they met with some opposition. While crossing the Mariager Fjord shortly after 1600 hrs, flak opened up and one of the No 234 Sqn aircraft flown by Plt Off Peter Bell was hit, wounding the pilot and forcing him to belly land near Hornum. He was immediately taken to the hospital, where he spent a brief period as a PoW. Escorting the Banff Wing Mosquitos that same day, No 19 Sqn suffered a double tragedy when the aircraft of Flt Lt 'Jock' Davidson and Kiwi Plt Off 'Baz' Natta collided over Denmark and they were both killed.

No 126 Sqn also flew its final war sorties during the day when it sortied a dozen Mustang III/IVs to escort Beaufighters attacking targets in the southern Kattegat. The squadron was led by Arne Austeen, its Norwegian CO, and diving down to strafe a U-boat his aircraft was hit by return fire from the submarine and blew up. The remainder of the formation landed at Lüneburg and then returned to Bentwaters the next day. Austeen's loss was the last suffered by an ace in an RAF Mustang in combat, and coming so close to war's end it was therefore particularly poignant.

Although the German unconditional surrender came into effect on 7 May 1945, the missions flown three days earlier were not the last operational flights made by RAF Mustang III/IVs. On 9 May several squadrons, led by the Hunsdon Wing leader Wg Cdr 'Jas' Storrar (flying his personal mount KM232/JAS), provided air cover for the reoccupation of the Channel Islands. After they had landed back in England, the significant part played by the Mustang III/IV in the RAF's campaign over Europe was indeed over.

On the historic final mission on 9 May 1945, Storrar flew his personal aircraft, KM232/JAS (*A J Mallandaine*)

APPENDICES

Commonwealth Mustang Aces

Name	Service	Unit/s	Mustang Claims	Total Claims	Theatre
Pinches M H	RAF	122	5+3sh/-/7	5+3sh/-/7	UK
Vassiliades B M	RAF	19	5+2sh/1/-	9+2sh/1	UK
Johnston G R A M	RAF	65, 122 Wg	5+2sh/-/2	9+2sh/2/2	UK
Lamb D P	RAF	19, 65	3+4sh/-/3	5+4sh/-/4	UK
Horbaczewski E	Polish	315	5+1sh/-/-	16+1sh/1/1	UK
Burra-Robinson L A P	RAF	122, 65, 61 OTU	5+1sh/-/3	5+1sh/-/3	UK
Collyns B G	RAF	65	4+2sh/1/3	5+2sh/1/3	UK
Pavey A F	RAF	122	4+2sh/1/1	4+3sh/1/6	UK
Pietrzak H J	Polish	306, 315, 309	4+2sh/-/1 4+1sh V1	7+2sh/-/2 4+1sh V1	UK
Potocki W J	Polish	306, 315, 309	4+2sh/-/-	4+2sh/-/1	UK
Hearne P J	RAF	65, 19	5/1/1	5/1/4	UK
Bargielowski J	Polish	315, 303	5/-/3 1+2sh V1	5/-/3 1+2sh V1	UK
Bell M H	RAAF	19	4+1sh/-/-	4+1sh/-/-	UK
Peglar W B**	RCAF	354th FS	4/-/- 1 on gnd	4/-/- 1 on gnd	UK

Commonwealth Aces with some Mustang Claims

Name	Service	Unit/s	Mustang Claims	Total Claims	Theatre
Jonsson T E	Icelandic	65	4/-/2	8/1/2	UK
Christie W	Norwegian	234, Hunsdon Wg	4/-/1	9+1sh/1/4+1sh	UK
Maclachlan J A F	RAF	AFDU	3+1sh/-/-	16+1sh/-/3	UK
Page A G	RAF	AFDU	2+1sh/-/-	10+5sh/-/3	UK
Talalla C L F	RAF	122	2+1sh/-/1	3+2sh/-/1	UK
Westenra D F	RAF	65	2+1sh/-/-	8+3sh/2/4	UK
Wonnacott G	RCAF	414	1+2sh/-/-	4+2sh/-/-	UK
Thorne J N	RAF	122	2/-/3	4+2sh/1sh/4	UK
Gilmour W M	RAF	239, 19	2/-/2	9/3/3	UK
Skalski S	Polish	133 Wg	2/-/-	24/1/5	UK
Sollogub G	Polish	306	2/-/-	5/1/-	UK
Loud W W J*	RAF	19	2/-/-	3+1sh/2/2	UK
Cwyner M	Polish	315, 316	1+1sh/-/- & 3 V1	5+1sh/1/- & 3 V1	UK
Blok S	Polish	315	1/-/1	5/1/3	UK
Sporny K	Polish	306	1/-/1	5/1/1	UK
Joyce E L	RNZAF	122	1/-/-	10/2/3	UK
Hills H H	RCAF	414	1/-/-	5/1/-	UK
Rutkowski K	Polish	133 Wg	1sh/1/-	5+1sh/2/1	UK
Hancock A J	RAF	129	1sh/-/-	5+2sh/3/2	UK
Crawford H A*	RCAF	14	1sh/-/-	2+1sh/-/-	ItBal
Zumbach J E L	Polish	133 Wg	-/1/-	12+2sh/5/1	UK
Wickham P R W	RAF	4th FG(attd), 122 Wg, Peterhead Wg	-/-/1	10/7/15	UK
Dalglish J B	RCAF	613	-/-/1	8+2sh/-/6+1sh	UK
Giddings K C M	RAF	118, 129	-/-/1sh	4+1sh/1/5	UK
Ruchwaldy D F	RAF	129	8 & 1sh V1	7/3/6 & 8+1sh V1	UK
Wunsche K	Polish	315	3 & 1sh V1	4+1sh/1/4 & 1sh V1	UK
Doyle J J	RCAF	101 IDF/AF	1/-/-	5/1/4	Israel (post-war)

Commonwealth Aces who flew Mustangs but made no Claims

Name	Service	Unit/s	Total Claims	Theatre
Arthur C I R	RAF	239 Wg	2+4sh/-/2	ItBal
Austeen A	Norwegian	122, 126	5+1sh/-/3	UK
Barwell E G	RAF	FIU	9/1/1 & 1 V1	UK
Bird-Wilson H A C	RAF	Bentwaters Wg	3+6sh/3/3	UK
Birksted K	Danish	Bentwaters Wg	10+1sh/-/5	UK
Crew E D	RAF	96	11+1sh/-/5 & 21 V1	UK
Currant C F	RAF	122 Wg	10+5sh/2/12	UK
Denholm G	RAF	?	3+3sh/3+1sh/6	UK
Doe R T F	RAF	613	14+2sh/-/5	UK
Drobinski B H	Polish	303	7/1+1sh/-	UK
Falkowski J P	Polish	Peterhead Wg	9/1/-	UK
Farnes P C P	RAF	611	7+2sh/2/11	UK
Gaze F AO	RAF	268	11+3sh/4/5	UK
Glowaki A	Polish	356th FS, 309th FG	8+1sh/3/5	UK
Griffiths G	RAF	4	5+5sh/3/1+1sh	UK
Haw C*	RAF	129	4/-/1+1sh	UK
Heppell P W *	RAF	118	4/1+1sh/5	UK
Jameson P G	RAF	122 Wg	9/1+1sh/2	UK
Jeka J	Polish	306	8/-/4	UK
Kimball D H	RCAF	441	6/-/-	UK
Lanowski W*	Polish	356th FS	4/-/-	UK
Llewellyn R T	RAF	112	13+1sh/1/2	ItBal
Lokuciewski W	Polish	303	8/3+1sh/-	UK
Longley H W *	RAF	FIU	2+1sh/-/-	UK
Maciejowski M M	Polish	309	10+1sh/1/1	UK
Nelson-Edwards G H	RAF	41 OTU, 231	1+4sh/3+1sh/8	UK
Nowierski T	Polish	133 Wg	5/2/5+1sh	UK
Parsonson J E	SAAF	8 SAAF Wg	4+1sh/-/3	ItBal
Plagis J A	RAF	126, Bentwaters Wg	15+2sh/2+2sh/6+1sh	UK
Plisnier A M	Belgian	336th FS	3+3sh/1/3	UK
Rudland C P*	RAF	64, Andrews Field Wg	2/-/-	UK
Sanders J G	RAF	41 OTU	16/1/6	UK
Scott A H	RAF	122	6+1sh/2/2	UK
Shaw J T	RAF	122	6+1sh/2/2	UK
Storrar J A	RAF	64, 165, 234, Hunsdon Wg, Molesworth Wg, 239 Wg	12+2sh/2+1sh/3	UK, ItBal
Thompson P D	RAF	129	2+3sh/2/-	UK
Urwin-Mann J R	RAF	85 GSU, 61 OTU	8+2sh/2/2	UK
Walker D R	RAF	-	4+1sh/-/2+1sh	UK
Westlake G H	RAF	239 Wg	9+2sh/1/3	ItBal
Wilmot L A	SAAF	239 Wg	4+1sh/-/-	ItBal

Mustang V1 Aces

Name	Service	Unit/s	Mustang Claims	Total Claims
Barlomiejczyk C	Polish	316	6 V1	1/-/- & 6 V1
Beyer A	Polish	306	1+2sh/-/- & 5 V1	1+2sh/-/- & 5 V1
Cholajda A	Polish	316	2/-/- & 6 V1	2/1/2 & 6 V1
Edwards E W	RAF	129	2/-/3 & 6 V1	2/-/3 & 6 V1
Hartley J	RAF	129	12 V1	12 V1
Jankowski T	Polish	315	2+1sh/-/- & 4+6sh V1	2+1sh/-/1 & 4+6sh V1
Karnrowski S	Polish	316	1+1sh/-/- & 2+3sh V1	1+1sh/1/- & 2+3sh V1
Klawe W	Polish	306	4+2sh V1	1/2/- & 4+2sh V1
Kleinmayer R G	RNZAF	129	7+1sh V1	7+1sh V1
Majewski L	Polish	316	5+1sh V1	1sh/-/- & 5+1sh V1
Mielnecki J A	Polish	316	6+1sh V1	6+1sh V1
Nowoczyn W	Polish	306	1/-/1 & 5 V1	1/-/1 & 5 V1
Osborne A F	RAF	129	4+2sh V1	1sh/-/- & 4+2sh V1
Pietrzak A	Polish	316, 309	2+1sh/-/1 & 4+1sh V1	3+1sh/-/2 & 4+1sh V1
Redhead E	RAF	129	6+1sh V1	6+1sh V1
Rogowski J	Polish	306	3+2sh V1	2/-/- & 3+2sh V1
Rudowski S	Polish	306	1/-/1 & 9+2sh V1	2/-/1 & 9+2sh V1
Siekierski S	Polish	306, 315	1/-/1 & 7+3sh V1	1/-/1 & 7+3sh V1
Siwek K	Polish	315	3/-/- & 6+2sh V1	3/-/- & 6+2sh V1
Swiston G	Polish	315	2+1sh/1/- & 1+5sh V1	2+1sh/1/- & 1+5sh V1
Szymankiewicz T	Polish	316	6 V1	1sh/-/- & 6 V1
Szymanski T	Polish	316	8 V1	2/1/- & 8 V1
Zalenski J	Polish	306	9+1sh V1	9+1sh V1

Notable Commonwealth Thunderbolt Pilots

Name	Service	Unit/s	Thunderbolt and P-47 Claims	Total Claims	Theatre
Gladych B M	Polish	61st FS	10/-/-	18/1/1sh	UK
Cameron N	RAF	258	1sh/-/-	3+2sh/1+1sh/1	FE
Lanowski W*	Polish	61st FS	4/-/-	4/-/-	UK
Carey F R	RAF	73 OTU	-	25+3sh/3/8	Egypt
Hawkins L C C	RAF	135	-	2/2/1	FE
Kilmartin J I	RAF	910 Wg, AHQ East Indies	-	13+2sh/-/1	FE
Glowczynski C	Polish	390th FS	-	5+2sh/2/1	UK
Yates J N	RAF	AFTU	-	4+2sh/2/2	FE

Notes

Those pilots with less than five victories are marked thus * and are shown because of their inclusion in *Aces High* or *Those other Eagles* where there may be doubt as to their actual scores. Those marked ** are included as the US Eighth Air Force gave ground claims the same status as aerial victories, thus making pilots who claimed five or more strafing kills aces

Theatre Abbreviations

UK - United Kingdom and Northwest Europe
ItBal - Mediterranean, Italy and the Balkans
FE - India, Burma and Southeast Asia

1

Mustang I AG470/RU-M of Flg Off H Hills, No 414 Sqn RCAF, Croydon, 19 August 1942

The first victory claimed by a Mustang pilot was appropriately made by an American serving with the RCAF, Flg Off Hollis Hills of No 414 Sqn, who was flying this aircraft. The Mustang Is were used on army co-operation duties, and it was during one such mission in support of the large scale raid on Dieppe that Hills gained his niche in history. In addition to a maple leaf badge, this aircraft also carried an animal's (wolf?) head in white under the cockpit. This was Hills' only victory with the RCAF, but he later transferred to the US Navy and became an ace flying F6F Hellcats in the Pacific in 1944. His mount survived the war and was eventually scrapped in 1947.

2

Mustang IA FD442 of Sqn Ldr J A F Maclachlan, AFDU, Duxford, 29 June 1943

James Maclachlan had achieved acedom over Malta but had lost his left arm in combat and been evacuated to the UK. He gained further victories before he began flying the Mustang I with the Air Fighting Development Unit. On 29 June 1943, in company with Flt Lt Geoffrey Page, he flew this aircraft on a low-level intruder sortie over France, where they encountered a formation of enemy Hs 126 army co-operation aircraft, two of which he shot down. A few miles further on they spotted a pair of Ju 88s, one of which Maclachlan also promptly destroyed and the pair then shared the other. These took the one-armed ace's final score to 16.5 kills. However, on 18 July, once more flying FD442, he was probably hit by ground fire and crash-landed, but died of his injuries a short while later.

3

Mustang III FB113/QV-H of Flt Lt D P Lamb, No 19 Sqn, Gravesend, 15 February 1944

FB113 was one of the first Mustang IIIs to be issued to a fighter unit, and it was flown by Flt Lt Deryck Lamb on No 19 Sqn's first operation on 15 February 1944 – a sweep over Holland and northern France. It became his regular aircraft, and Lamb's next operation in it was to support a raid by USAAF B-26s. He also flew FB113 on the evening of D-Day, escorting transport aircraft to their drop zones near Caen. Four days later Lamb was at its controls when he damaged a Bf 109. He damaged another ten days later, when he also shared in the destruction of an Fw 190. On 21 June Lamb destroyed a Bf 109 and on 8 July he shared in the destruction of two more, which took him to acedom. Like Lamb, FB113 also survived the war.

4

Mustang III FZ120/YT-J of Sqn Ldr D H Westenra, No 65 Sqn, Ford and Funtington, April-May 1944

A successful ace from North Africa, New Zealand-born Sqn Ldr 'Jerry' Westenra became the CO of No 65 Sqn in March 1944, at which point FZ120 became his regular mount. The fighter's spinner is thought to have been painted red, but otherwise it wore standard markings for the period. Westenra claimed his first Mustang III victories over Denmark in May,

although it is uncertain if it was in this aircraft. However, he was certainly flying FZ120 on 8 June, by which time it was adorned with broad black and white 'D-Day' stripes. That day, when in a combat during a bombing attack near Dreux, Westenra shot down an Fw 190 to take his final total to eight and three shared destroyed. He left the unit the following month. FZ120 wore the squadron badge on the nose and later served with several Polish units.

5

Mustang III FB125/DV-F of Flt Lt D F Ruchwaldy, No 129 Sqn, Coolham, April-May 1944

FB125 was one of the longest serving Merlin-Mustangs, having flown on No 129 Sqn's first operation on 26 April 1944 when the unit flew a 'Ranger' to Beauvais. It also participated in the squadron's final combat operation too on 20 April 1945 – an extraordinarily long time for a frontline fighter in World War 2, although from 25 August it became DV-C. During mid-1944 it was the regular mount of Flt Lt Desmond Ruchwaldy, who flew it on 22 May during a 'Ramrod' against engine sheds at Monceau-sur-mer. FB125 was also flown by the leading Mustang V1 ace, Flg Off James Hartley, who on 19 August downed two flying bombs near Dymchurch with it. Ruchwaldy was also successful against the V1s, destroying ten of them – his only claims in the Mustang III.

6

Mustang III FZ190/QV-A at WO M H Bell, No 19 Sqn, Funtington, 9 May 1944

The only RAAF pilot to achieve five victories with the Mustang III was Max Bell, a 21-year-old Queenslander who flew this aircraft on an uneventful sweep to Metz, in eastern France, on 9 May 1944. The previous day it had been flown by another future Mustang III ace, Flt Sgt Basilios Vassiliades, on a dive-bombing mission. Bell's first success came soon afterwards when he shared in the destruction of a LeO 451 near Aalborg, and in the days after D-Day he claimed three enemy fighters. On 19 August Bell shot down another to make his fifth claim, but during a ground strafe in early September he was hit by flak and taken prisoner, subsequently being executed. FZ190 fared better, having a long career and finally being scrapped post-war.

7

Mustang III FB201/QV-D of Sqn Ldr W M Gilmour, No 19 Sqn, Funtington, 29 May 1944

FB201 was flown by a number of aces during its service with No 19 Sqn, most notably the CO, seven-victory ace Sqn Ldr 'Mac' Gilmour. It became his regular aircraft, flying it for the first time on a sweep to Cambrai on 29 May. He also flew FB201 on the evening of D-Day during a mission in support of an airborne drop. Gilmour used the fighter on 20 June to achieve his first success with the Mustang III when, near Dreux, he shot down a Bf 109 and damaged another. Four days later Flt Sgt Vassiliades was at the controls of FB201 when he destroyed an Fw 190 and a Bf 109, thus becoming an ace. Gilmour claimed his ninth, and final, victory in FB201 near Caen on 12 July, shooting down a Bf 109. The aircraft was subsequently lost the following month whilst being flown by another pilot.

8

Mustang III FB169/DV-H of Sqn Ldr C Haw, No 129 Sqn, Coolham, 6 June 1944

When No 129 Sqn converted to the Mustang III, FB169 became the regular mount of the CO, Sqn Ldr 'Wag' Haw, who had been the RAF's most successful pilot in Russia in 1941. On 29 April Haw took part in a wing sweep to the Coulomiers area, and he flew it again on his next operation – a sweep to the Reims-Paris area on 22 May, when he led eight 'bombers' and four escorts on a 'Ramrod' to the locomotive sheds at Monceau-sur-mer. Haw was also flying it, as depicted here in broad AEAF identity stripes, when, on the evening of 6 June, he led 11 aircraft as cover to a drop by airborne forces landing in the eastern beach area. However, one week later, when taxiing on the rough strip at Coolham, a bomb dropped off FB169's wing, wrecking the fighter.

9

Mustang III FZ196/UZ-D of Flt Lt W Potocki, No 306 Sqn, Coolham, 7 June 1944

One of the most successful Polish pilots on the Mustang III was Wladislaw Potocki, who claimed six victories (two of them shared) on the type. He had a long tour flying with No 306 Sqn, and during June 1944 Potocki regularly flew FZ196. Indeed, he was in it during his second patrol on D+1 when, at around 1800 hrs between Argentan and Caen, his flight encountered some enemy fighters and he shot down two Bf 109s. FZ196 was successful again on the 17th, this time in the hands of WO Pomietlarz, who shared an Fw 190 with Potocki – the latter 'made ace' a week later. On 27 September FZ196 crashed during a 'Ramrod' to Holland following an engine failure, killing Flt Sgt Koloszczyk.

10

Mustang III FB145/PK-F of Flt Sgt J Bargielowski, No 315 Sqn, Coolham, 12 June 1944

Jakub Bargielowski joined No 315 Sqn in early 1944 and converted to Mustang IIIs with the unit in the spring. He flew FB145 on a number of occasions, including 12 June on a 'Ramrod' by four aircraft to the Argentan-Vire area of Normandy. A few miles to the south of Caen they had a fight with seven Fw 190s and Bargielowski shot down two, so beginning his road to acedom – he achieved this later in the year. FB145 remained with No 315 Sqn until it was transferred to the Middle East, while its pilot, having been promoted to warrant officer, also survived the war.

11

Mustang III FB226/MT-K of Flg Off C L F Talalla, No 122 Sqn, Ford, 12 June 1944

Twenty-three-year-old 'Jimmy' Talalla was of Singhalese extraction from Malaya, and he had gained his first victories flying Spitfires with No 118 Sqn in 1943. He joined No 122 Sqn as flight commander for a second tour, and shortly after D-Day on the evening of 12 June he flew FB226, as shown here, on an armed reconnaissance and bombed a train at La Queue les Yuelines, recording two near misses. It was not his regular mount, and Talalla next flew it on 17 August, by which

time the AEAF stripes had been removed from the uppersurfaces, to attack barges on the Seine – a mission that he repeated again the following day. His final flight in FB226 was on the 26th when he flew an armed reconnaissance to the Amiens area, during which he attacked some motorised transport. Talalla achieved ace status four weeks later.

12

Mustang III FZ114/MT-A of Flg Off M H Pinches, No 122 Sqn, Ford, 17 June 1944

The most successful Commonwealth pilot on the Mustang III was Maurice Pinches, a former RAF apprentice, and he achieved most of his success at the controls of this aircraft. On 17 May he was flying it on the very successful 'Ranger' to Aalborg where he began his road to acedom by shooting down an He 177 and Ju 188, as well as sharing in the destruction of a hapless W 34 – he also damaged two Ar 196 floatplanes as they sat at their moorings. At the time of D-Day FZ114 had AEAF stripes painted on it, and the fighter had also acquired a coloured spinner. It was thus coloured late on 17 June when Pinches had a fight with a Bf 109 south of Dreux and shot it down. He continued to fly FZ114 over the next month, and on 15 July achieved ace status in it when he shared another Ju 188. Ten days later Pinches had his final success in FZ114 when, near Evreux, he destroyed an Fw 190 and damaged two more. Sadly, during the autumn he contracted jaundice and died in late October. FZ114 was shot down by flak near Fecamp on the evening of 24 August.

13

Mustang III FB260/LW of Lt Col L A Wilmot, No 239 Wing, Falerium and Iesi, Italy, June-August 1944

Many of the Mustang IIIs delivered to the Mediterranean were fitted with the original framed cockpit cover as evident on FB260, which was the personal mount of the leader of No 239 Wing in Italy, Lt Col Laurie Wilmot. As entitled by his position, Wilmot's aircraft carries his initials in place of the unit codes. He was one of a number of highly capable wing leaders from the SAAF that led RAF formations, and on completion of his tour Wilmot received a DSO. FB260 also survived the conflict to be scrapped post-war.

14

Mustang III FB337/AK-A of Sqn Ldr S R Whiting, No 213 Sqn, Leverano, Italy, July 1944

Spencer Whiting, CO of No 213 Sqn, achieved all six of his claims in FB337 when leading his unit in the summer of 1944. During a sweep over Croatia on 15 July they encountered a formation of Bucker biplanes, and Whiting claimed two destroyed. Five days later, on another sweep, his section attacked a formation of Hs 126s and their Bf 109 escorts, and in the ensuing combat Whiting made four claims – a Bf 109 destroyed and another as a probable, as well as a Henschel destroyed and another damaged. He left the unit in the autumn, whilst FB337 was shot down by flak in October.

15

P-51B Mustang 42-106950/WR-P of Flt Lt W B Peglar, 354th FS/355th FG, Steeple Morden, July-August 1944

Warren Peglar was one of a number of experienced RAF and Commonwealth pilots seconded to the USAAF's Eighth Air

Force in mid-1944. Attached to the 355th FG's 354th FS, he flew this P-51C, christened *The Iowa Beaut*, three times, despite it being the usual aircraft of his friend 1Lt Robert E Huldeman. Boasting ten victory symbols, the fighter was lost over Germany on 11 September while being flown by Capt Kevin G Rafferty. Peglar's missions included some that landed in the USSR, and he shot down four enemy fighters during his attachment to the 354th FS. He also destroyed a solitary Ju 52/3m on the ground, so becoming an ace in the Eighth Air Force. Peglar was the most successful RCAF Mustang pilot.

16

Mustang III HB886/TN of Grp Capt T Nowierski, No 133 (Polish) Wing, Brenzett, August 1944

The CO of the Polish Mustang Wing from July 1944, Tadeusz Nowierski had achieved his five victories flying Spitfires. He was allocated HB886 as his personal mount, and it wore the usual markings for the period, including the Polish check on the nose. As was his privilege, it also bore Nowierski's initials. He made his sole Mustang III claim in HB886 when, near Arnhem during a 'Ramrod' on 5 August, he spotted a V1 that was probably heading for Antwerp and shot it down. Nowierski remained in command until February 1945, while HB886 served with several Polish units and survived the war.

17

Mustang III HB936/GA-A of Sgt A Banks, No 112 Sqn, Iesi, Italy, 29 August 1944

With their ferocious looking sharksmouth marking on the nose, the aircraft of No 112 Sqn were probably the most distinctive Mustang IIIs to serve with the RAF. However, by the time the unit had received them in mid-1944 there was little enemy air activity in Italy, and they were employed mainly on ground attack work. Among the unit's pilots was Sgt Arthur Banks, who on 29 August flew this aircraft on an armed reconnaissance of the Ravenna and Ferrara areas. He was hit and force-landed, but managed to join an Italian partisan group and played a key part in their activities until his capture. Interrogated and brutally tortured over several days by his captors, Banks was eventually shot. When his incredible courage and fortitude became known, he was posthumously awarded the George Cross.

18

Mustang III HB952/GN-F of Sqn Ldr J te Kloot, No 249 Sqn, Canne, Italy, 28 September 1944

Although he made no air-to-air claims, No 249 Sqn CO Jack te Kloot took a heavy toll of enemy aircraft during strafing attacks. Flying this aircraft on 28 September 1944, he led a highly profitable attack on Salonika airfield, where he personally destroyed a Ju 52/3m, an Italian aircraft and an He 111, as well as damaging a Go 242 glider. Later in the mission his aircraft took a cannon hit in the wing, and he was lucky to return. This ended a very successful week for him, as in two sorties over Greece a few days earlier he had destroyed five more Ju 52/3ms. At the end of his tour Jack te Kloot was awarded the DSO.

19

Thunderbolt I HB975/WK-L of Sqn Ldr L C C Hawkins, No 135 Sqn, Chittagong, India, October-December 1944

When No 135 Sqn re-equipped with Thunderbolts its CO was Sqn Ldr Lee Hawkins who, over Burma, had made a total of five claims, including two destroyed. He adopted HB975 as his personal aircraft, and he regularly flew it on operations until April 1945. The first time was on 18 October 1944, when he led a four-ship formation against a ground target. Hawkins also flew it on long-range escort missions for bombing raids on the Rangoon area, including on 3 November when the JAAF was encountered, although he was unable to increase his score. Hawkins was again at the fighter's controls three weeks later when he escorted an attack on the notorious Burma-Siam railway. HB975 was scrapped in May 1945.

20

Mustang III FB344/AZ-Z of Maj W H Christie, No 234 Sqn, Bentwaters, January-February 1945

Werner Christie was one of the most successful Norwegian aces, and he became one of several to command an RAF unit when in December 1944 he became the CO of No 234 Sqn. During his brief tenure he flew this aircraft most frequently, Christie having had its spinner painted red for easier recognition. On 9 February he flew on a mission over Germany, and having strafed some transports on the ground, he then spotted three Ar 96 trainers practising air combat over Treuchtlingen. The Mustang IIIs duly joined in, and he shot down one of the Arados to claim the first of his four Mustang III/IV victories. Christie left to command the Hunsdon Wing a few days later, but his successor, and fellow ace, Sqn Ldr 'Jas' Storrar flew FB344 on his first trip on 14 February. The fighter was later transferred to No 64 Sqn.

21

Mustang IV KH681/GL-Z of Capt H J E Clarke, No 5 Sqn SAAF, Fano, Italy, December 1944-January 1945

Capt 'Nobby' Clarke, who had three victories on Kittyhawks, joined No 5 Sqn SAAF in November 1944, and he flew his first mission – a 'cab rank' patrol to the west of Faenza – on the morning of 15 December. KH681 was not his regular mount, however, although he flew it again in January 1945, initially on the 4th when he led an attack on a ground target. Clarke later became the squadron CO, and he was killed in action on No 5 Sqn SAAF's very last mission. KH681, which carried the distinctive orange-centred SAAF roundels, also wore a white fin top as an additional unit identifier. It was lost in action on 2 February 1945.

22

Thunderbolt II HD292/ZT-L of Sqn Ldr N Cameron, No 258 Sqn, Ratnap, India, 11 February 1945

The CO of No 258 Sqn, Sqn Ldr Neil Cameron, who had three and one shared victories to his name from service in the UK, Russia and North Africa, flew this aircraft on 11 February 1945 as escort to the heaviest bombing raid of the campaign in Burma to date. Six Ki-61s intercepted the bombers over the target, and one was attacked head on by Cameron, who initially only claimed it as a possible. However, he was subsequently credited with a half-share in its destruction. In thus being elevated to acedom, Cameron had made the only claim by an ace in an RAF Thunderbolt – and indeed the type's final victory in British colours. HD292 was his regular mount, and it briefly bore red and white checks on the nose, although these had been replaced by the usual white identity stripe by the time the aircraft was committed to action.

23
Mustang III KH570/5J-X of Maj A Austeen, No 126 Sqn, Bentwaters, 23 February 1945
Norwegian ace Arne Austeen claimed all of his victories flying Spitfires, but in February 1945 he was given command of the Mustang-equipped No 126 Sqn, which was part of the large Bentwaters Wing. On one of his first operations he flew KH570 on a long-range escort. Austeen led many more such missions, including the whole wing on 25 April when it provided the escort for an attack on Berchtesgaden – the last Bomber Command raid of the war. Another late war casualty, Austeen was killed on 4 May leading his unit in a sweep off Denmark, his Mustang III being hit by flak and exploding during an attack on a U-boat.

24
Mustang III KH503/NK-Z of Flt Lt K C M Giddings, No 118 Sqn, Bentwaters, 23 March 1945
Flt Lt Mike Giddings, who had earlier become an ace flying Spitfires with No 118 Sqn, made only one claim after the unit had re-equipped with the Mustang III. It was, however, a significant one. He was flying this aircraft, recorded as NK-Z and believed to be KH503, on a long-range bomber escort to a raid on Bremen on 23 March 1945 when his charges came under attack from a large group of Me 262s. Although the jets proved to be too fast for a decisive engagement, three of them were damaged by No 118 Sqn, one by Giddings, who saw strikes and structural damage on the starboard wing of his target. KH503 survived the war to be scrapped in 1947.

25
Mustang III KH574/WC-A of Sqn Ldr A Glowacki, No 309 Sqn, Andrews Field, April 1945
KH574, which had previously served with No 316 Sqn, was regularly flown by No 309 Sqn's CO and nine-victory ace 'Toni' Glowacki on long-range escort duties during the spring of 1945. He had briefly flown P-51Bs with the Eighth Air Force the previous year, and flew Mustang IIIs with No 309 Sqn until war's end. For its escort tasks KH574 routinely carried long-range tanks, and like its Polish brethren it bore the national red and white check marking on the nose. The aircraft was also flown on occasion by the No 133 Wing leader, Wg Cdr Kazimierez Rutowski.

26
Mustang IV KH860/AZ-G of Sqn Ldr J A Storrar, No 234 Sqn, Bentwaters, April 1945
The first Mustang IV arrived for No 234 Sqn during the tenure of Sqn Ldr 'Jas' Storrar, who had over a dozen victories. He first flew this aircraft, which retained its natural metal colour, on 18 April 1945 on an escort for 800+ bombers attacking Heligoland, following which he led his squadron on a sweep over Lübeck. Storrar used it again on the 19th and 20th too, escorting Lancasters in raids on Munich and Regensburg. He left the squadron soon afterwards, but KH860 did not last long for on 4 May, during an escort to coastal strike aircraft off Denmark when flown by Plt Off Bell, it was hit by flak and belly landed near Hornum, its pilot briefly becoming a PoW.

27
Mustang IV KH765/HG-R of Flt Lt N W Lee, No 154 Sqn, Hunsdon, March 1945
During two tours in the Mediterranean, Flt Lt Norm Lee made 14 combat claims, although only one was for an aircraft destroyed. On his third tour he flew Mustang IVs, piloting KH765 throughout March on bomber escort work. Lee made his only Mustang IV claim when flying this aircraft on the 27th. After leaving the bombers to sweep the Lübeck area, he ran into some Fw 190s and damaged one of them, which was also attacked by Plt Off Todd. After No 154 Sqn's disbandment, KH765 served with several other units.

28
Thunderbolt II KJ348 of Grp Capt F R Carey, No 73 OTU, Fayid, Egypt, spring 1945
Grp Capt Frank Carey was one of the RAF's most influential, and able, fighter leaders, having been posted in to command No 73 OTU from Burma in late 1944. It was his unit's responsibility to maintain the flow of fighter pilots to the Far East. At Fayid, Carey adopted KJ348 as his personal mount. It was painted in an all-black colour scheme with a broad red stripe down the fuselage to make him instantly recognisable in the air to any students unfortunate enough not to have spotted him. Despite the size and weight of the Thunderbolt, he occasionally demonstrated his skill and the type's capabilities to any doubters!

29
Mustang IV KM193/QV-J of Sqn Ldr P J Hearne, No 19 Sqn, Peterhead, April-May 1945
The last RAF pilot to become an ace with the Mustang III was Peter Hearne on 14 April 1945. A few days later he made his first Mk IV flight in KM193 on the 20th, exclaiming that it was 'a superb aircraft'. He flew his first operation in it on 2 May when he escorted 22 Mosquitos to the Kattegat, where they attacked two U-boats off the coast of Denmark. He was also in it two days later when he led No 19 Sqn's last operation of the war – another Mosquito escort. Unlike some of its brethren, KM193 lacked a striped spinner.

30
Mustang IV KH695/YT-E of Flt Lt G S Pearson, No 65 Sqn, 19 April 1945
On 19 April Mustang IV KH695/YT-E force-landed at Getteron, on the west coast of Sweden, after an engine failure during an escort mission over the Skagerrak when escorting Mosquitos of the Banff Wing. Its pilot, Flt Lt Graham Pearson, was interned. He had four victories and a probable – all on Mustangs. With three victories and a probable, Pearson is thought to have been the top-scoring RAF Mustang IV pilot. Unlike many other Mk IVs, KH695 was fully camouflaged.

31
Mustang IV KH826/AK-G of Flt Lt G S Hulse, No 213 Sqn, Biferno, Italy, 23 April 1945
The last air combat claim by the RAF in the Mediterranean theatre came on 23 April 1945 when Flt Lt Graham Hulse, flying his regular mount KH826, encountered a pair of Croatian Bf 109s. He fired and hit 'Black 14', but only claimed it as damaged, although in fact it crash-landed. This was the

last of Hulse's seven claims during World War 2 (although he claimed none destroyed). He went on to have several successes against MiG-15s when flying F-86s on exchange with the USAF during the Korean War. Post-war research suggests that like the Croatian Bf 109, another of Hulse's damaged claims was in fact shot down. His mount wears the fin identity band commonly seen on Mustangs in Italy.

32

Mustang IV KM121/MLD of Wg Cdr M L Donnet, Bentwaters Wing, Bentwaters, April 1945

Although not an ace, Wg Cdr Mike Donnet had nine claims, including three destroyed, and he was one of the leading Belgian pilots of the war. In February 1945 he was appointed wing leader of the Mustang III/IV-equipped Bentwaters Wing, which he successfully led on long-range escort missions. Like other wing leaders, he applied his initials to his personal aircraft, in this case KM121, although on 23 April he had the misfortune to suffer an engine failure in this machine, causing him to crash-land near Godalming, in Surrey. Post-war, Donnet rose to high rank in the Belgian Air Force, retiring as a lieutenant general.

33

Mustang IV KH729/Y2-A of Wg Cdr J A Storrar, No 442 Sqn, Hunsdon, 25 April 1945

KH729 was the usual mount of No 442 Sqn's CO, Sqn Ldr Mitchell Johnston, and he was flying it when his squadron made their only claims with the Mustang on 16 April. On the 25th it was flown by the Hunsdon Wing leader, Wg Cdr J A Storrar, when he led his wing as escort for the last raid by Bomber Command 'heavies' to Berchtesgaden. No 442 Sqn's last operational sorties were made on 9 May, when the unit covered the re-occupation of the Channel Islands. KH729 participated in this operation too, being flown by Flt Lt W V Shenk.

34

Mustang IV KH676/CV-A of Flg Off A F Lane, No 3 Sqn RAAF, Cervia, Italy, April 1945

In early April 1945 'Dusty' Lane claimed one of No 3 Sqn RAAF's few victories on the Mustang III/IV when he shot down an Fi 156 over Yugoslavia. He flew KH676 regularly throughout the latter part of the month, including twice on the 25th in attacks on canal lock gates. The following day Lane attacked a ferry crossing in it, despite being opposed by heavy flak. The Mustang III/IVs of No 3 Sqn RAAF proclaimed their Australian ownership by having their fins painted blue, onto which the unit applied the stars of the Southern Cross.

35

Mustang III HB876/9G-L of Flt Lt D H Kimball, No 441 Sqn RCAF, Digby, May 1945

No 441 Sqn did not re-equip with Mustang IIIs until the final days of the war, and it never became operational on them. One of the flight commanders was six-victory ace Flt Lt Don Kimball, who flew this aircraft on some of the squadron's first Mustang III familiarisation flights in late May. Unlike many of the others, HB876 was finished in natural metal. Soon afterwards Kimball went to Canada on leave and No 441 Sqn was disbanded later in the summer.

36

Mustang IV KM132/FY-S of Sqn Ldr P C P Farnes, No 611 'West Lancashire' Sqn, Peterhead, 27 July 1945

No 611 Sqn successfully flew Mustang IVs on escort operations through the spring of 1945, and Battle of Britain ace Sqn Ldr Paul Farnes took over as CO of the unit in mid-July, remaining until it disbanded a month later. During his time he flew KM132 on several occasions, including twice on 27 July on low-level flights that he described as 'exhilarating!'

BIBLIOGRAPHY

Bowyer, Michael, *Fighting Colours.* PSL, 1969 and 1975

Brown, Robin A, *Shark Squadron.* Crecy, 1994

Cull, Brian, *249 at War.* Grub St, 1997

Cull, Brian, *One Armed Mac.* Grub St, 2003

Delve, Ken, *The Mustang Story.* Arms and Armour, 1999

Donnet, Baron Michael, *Flight to Freedom.* Wingham Press, 1991

Fergusson, Aldon, *Beware, Beware.* Airfield Publications, 2004

Flintham, Vic and Thomas, Andrew, *Combat Codes.* Airlife, 2003 and 2008

Griffin, John and Kostenuk, Samuel, *RCAF Sqn Histories and Aircraft.* S Stevens, 1977

Halley, James, *Squadrons of the RAF and Commonwealth.* Air Britain, 1988

Hamlin, John, *Flat Out!* Air Britain, 2002

Jefford, Wg Cdr C G, *RAF Squadrons.* Airlife 1988 and 2001

Jonsson, Tony, *Dancing the Skies.* Grub St, 1994

Leeson, Frank, *The Hornet Strikes.* Air Britain, 1998

MacDonald, Capt Grant, *442 Sqn.* History, Private, 1987

Milberry, Larry and Halliday, Hugh, *The RCAF at War 1939-1945.* CANAV Books, 1990

Palmer, Derek, *Fighter Squadron.* Self Publishing, 1990

Rawlings, John D R, *Fighter Squadrons of the RAF.* Macdonald, 1969

Richards, Denis, *RAF Official History 1939-45, Parts 2 & 3.* HMSO, 1954

Scutts, Jerry, *P-47 Thunderbolt – The Operational Record.* Airlife, 1998

Shores, Christopher, *Those Other Eagles.* Grub St, 2004

Shores, Christopher and Thomas, Chris, *2nd Tactical Air Force Vols 1-4.* Classic Publications, 2004-2009

Shores, Christopher and Williams, Clive, *Aces High Vol 1.* Grub St, 1994

Shores, Christopher, *Aces High Vol 2.* Grub St, 1999

Walpole, Grp Capt Nigel, *Dragon Rampant.* Merlin Massara, 2007

ACKNOWLEDGEMENTS

The author wishes to record his gratitude to the following former Mustang and Thunderbolt pilots who have given of their time in presenting accounts or information for inclusion within this volume – Flt Lt E Andrews, Lt B Chiazzari SAAF, Flt Lt W Fleming, AVM W Harbison CB CBE AFC, the late Sqn Ldr C Haw DFC DFM OL, Sqn Ldr J te Kloot DSO, Flg Off P N G Knowles, Flt Lt A J Mallandaine RCAF, Sqn Ldr A S Murkowski, Flt Lt W B Peglar DFC RCAF and R T Williams DFM.

INDEX

References to illustrations are shown in **bold**.
Plates are shown with page and caption locators
in brackets.